Contents

Meet the author

Writing *Simple Steps to Positive Living* has been an inspiring, joyful and deeply thought-provoking time. Each day, as I've sat down to work, whatever my current mood or circumstances, positivity has started to flow as soon as I've started to write.

A positive attitude and thoughtful approach can lift us out of the shadows if we're feeling down and give us added gladness when all is well.

Increasingly as the years have gone by, I've realised that thinking positively is a choice we can make at any time. As soon as we take that positive step a special kind of energy starts to flow along with several other feel-good traits like love, courage, common sense and optimism.

Although thinking positively is habitual for me I'll still catch myself being negative sometimes, it is particularly difficult when I suffer hurt or bereavement for example. During these downtimes I try not to lose sight of the light of positivity. I know that all I have to do is allow the light back in, think positively, and I will be able to go on.

Above all, our positivity helps us see and participate in the goodness and wonder of life - so complex, so extraordinary, so full of goodness, beauty and love.

In sharing my experience, techniques and tips on positivity I hope to enable you to increase yours. It's an ongoing process but it feels wonderful!

Introduction

A sense of wonder and fizz. Every day a new exciting proposition; life full of promise and potential. We live it often when we are children. Then again, if we are lucky, when we fall in love. And now and again throughout our lives it's there in certain moments of happiness and joy, wonder and awe. Wouldn't it be amazing to have that feeling just about every day? And in between to be full of energy, calm and confident that all is or will be well, knowing we can limit and find our way through any patches of negativity.

Such feel-good positivity is a natural part of being alive. But along the way we all inevitably have disappointments and sorrows, pressures and stress that can push our natural happiness down or even under in various degrees of depression. We're even taught by others to suppress our confidence, optimism and exuberance. One way or another, life isn't always what we thought it would be.

The great news is that yes it's still possible to live in the light of positivity and feel its amazing energy. Whatever your age, whatever you've been through, whatever happens in future, life can be good, really good.

I can't wave a magic wand and promise that reading this book will transform your life because of course it's up to you to do the transforming. But I will tell you everything I know that will show you the way and lead you along it – a way of light and love where enthusiasm trumps apathy, and courage along with your innate ability deals constructively with fear.

It's a way of being where gladness becomes your default setting and, whatever is or isn't happening in your life, you feel loved. And I can promise that if you decide to take the journey and you live the positive way – really live it that is, not faking, not pretending but becoming and being positive in mind, body and spirit – you will know yourself better than you ever have and love this wonderful person you truly are. You'll feel you've found the place you've always longed for – your purpose in this astonishing world and a deep contentment in belonging here – and you'll appreciate every precious moment of your life in both the good and bad times.

You'll have the pleasure of being at home – at home with yourself and in your immediate environment, in your relationships and local community and in the world as a whole. You'll know you *do* make a difference. And whatever your thoughts and beliefs on this universe being all there is, or a part of something far greater, you'll feel in touch with the mystery and with the power of love.

It's your personal story, about you, your life and your positive power. This combination of emotional, mental and spiritual strength is unique to you, supports you, and lets your natural abilities, personality and inner beauty open your eyes to the full spectrum of joy.

I don't want to only show you the joy of positivity – I want you to feel it for yourself in all sorts of ways, finding something that speaks directly to you in every chapter – perhaps every page. You can read it right through or dip in and out at different places. I find that with the books that have been stars of light for me I can open them at random and serendipitously – or perhaps, who knows, drawn there by something we don't yet understand – find something hugely helpful and positive for that precise moment of my life. I hope that happens to you with this book. I hope you feel and absorb the energy and love and sheer, heartfelt, spirit-led inspiration with which I'm writing it.

For anyone reading this who feels the light has gone out or is dim in their life just now, I hope this inspiration turns the lights back on or up for you. It has happened to me at times and I feel for you and cheer you on as you grasp the lifeline of positivity. For those of you who are already pretty positive and enjoy life, I hope it encourages you to appreciate it to the full and constantly renew the wonder.

I want all of us to shine. As Marianne Williamson wrote and Nelson Mandela repeated: 'We are all meant to shine.'

Being positive lets us do just that. Let's go for it.

You have huge reserves of ability and love. Use far, far more of it and make your life – and the world – not just a better place but an enjoyable, beautiful, positively wondrous place to be.

In your own way, shine!

1

Attitude!

In this chapter, you'll embrace positivity when you:
- *Recognize your ability to choose a positive attitude*
- *Improve relationships and understanding with an all-round perspective and clear perception*
- *Use body language to reflect and increase your positivity*
- *Decide positively whether to stay in neutral or active gear*
- *Touch your own and others' lives with your* joie de vivre
- *Let positivity guide you*
- *Enjoy small everyday pleasures*
- *Review your personal attitude recipe*
- *Let your energy trigger and resonate with other people's*
- *Love your work*
- *Transform failure into success*
- *Remember to resist others' negativity*
- *Travel through life with openness, optimism and eyes wide open to beauty, wonder and love.*

It all starts with a positive attitude. Think positive and in the blink of an eye you feel better. It's also a catalyst for a joyful outlook and plenty of energy. It opens up a new path through life, a way of being that feels right for you. Whatever kind of personality you have, positivity will complement it. Life can be as calm and quiet or as busy and bouncy as you wish – it's your call completely.

Positivity is always there for you, even in the darkest corners. When you choose a positive stance you invite and enable or accentuate all sorts of positive aspects of your life. You'll experience the feel-good emotions like love, happiness and optimism more often and more deeply too. You'll also realize you can do a lot of the things you've always wanted to and make them a part of your life. Altogether you'll enjoy your work and leisure time more too. It's a lot to do with energy. Positivity has its own innate energy and with a positive attitude you let it flow and keep it recharged.

A positive attitude is strong, exciting and full of warmth and light – and it's your choice every moment, every day.

Choose a positive attitude

Everything we do we can choose to do positively. Whatever happens to us, we can work out how to react as positively as possible. Positivity is a wonderful way of being that lets our energy flow and enables us to enjoy life to the full.

Taking a positive attitude makes an extraordinarily beneficial impact on our lives and yet all it takes is a subtle shift of consciousness – a tiny quantum leap that feels good every time and gets easier and easier the more you practise.

We react to every experience we have in life emotionally, logically and with behaviour that reflects both of these. Our reactions are steered from day one by our parents and other carers. From them we learn what is, in their view, good and bad, safe and dangerous. Most of us learn early on that it's fine to smile, laugh and enjoy life – all of which come very naturally to us. Think of the chuckle of a baby or toddler – it's one of the most wonderfully positive sounds and sights of the world – just joyous.

Being in positive mode as an adult feels great too and will do so all our lives through if we give it a chance. And every step of the way we can choose to do that, just as we so naturally did as kids.

It doesn't matter if the school of life taught us to be negative a lot of the time – for some, sadly, *all* the time – because now it's *you* who is your principle carer, your inspiration, your head teacher, your current mentor. You don't have to follow anyone else because you have the wherewithal to make your own choices about how you react, feel and behave. You can choose the attitude you want to take to everything that happens to you. You can reclaim positivity as your natural way of being. It's your choice and your absolute right to have a positive outlook and it will release your personal power and bring you joy that lights up your life.

It isn't about putting on a mask or pretending to be something you're not. We all have the ability to register the emotional impact of something and adjust the way we react. It's hugely empowering just to realize this. For if you choose to react positively, you will automatically feel more positive.

Pause to consider, just for a moment, how good it is that you will no longer be at the mercy of negative drives and that you have the power to be rational and in command of your equanimity.

Positivity gives you access to your reserves of energy and strength and keeps them topped up – constantly replenishing, always vibrant. And it's life, love and happiness affirming too.

Some treat positivity and the happiness with which it goes hand in hand like a holy grail – something that you can spend a lifetime searching for and which you rarely capture. But it's not even elusive. It's there for you right now and always. It's your choice in every moment. Yes, it's challenging because it requires your attention and resolve. And it's very exciting because it opens up all sorts of possibilities, releases previously unexplored potential and opens your eyes to all kinds of goodness and love in the world around you that you may not previously have been aware of. But it's not difficult – in fact once you get into the habit of positive thinking it's far easier than being negative. There are five steps to knowing you can choose a positive attitude:

1 Remember you have the choice of how to react.
2 Pause in your mind.
3 Breathe deeply and slowly.
4 Ask yourself: How am I going to react to this - what is the positive attitude?
5 Now ask yourself: What is the positive way forward?

The potentially challenging bit about thinking positively, when we've had years of thinking that being negative is the right and/or only way to be, is remembering that you have the choice of how to react. The other steps follow more naturally. All of them feel good because having control of your life, your being and your positivity feels good in itself.

If things aren't going your way just now, or even if they feel bleak, a positive stance will help you cope so life feels better. But it doesn't end there. Thinking positively will impact on your mood and your behaviour, changing the way you feel, speak and act. This in turn – and it can happen in an instant – has an effect on other people and the world around you. You only have to try it to experience the uplift you get and how you can beneficially influence situations.

What matters is that you can sense the energy of positivity, see it, use it and gloriously, joyfully discover it right now, for yourself.

It could be something of a revelation if you find life a bit of a struggle, plain disappointing or somehow not as interesting and as much fun as you feel it could be. The discovery that by thinking positively your personal energy will transcend all of that and turn your life into a good, interesting, more comfortable and often enthralling place to be is for many an astonishing idea. Actually it still wows me the way it works – that our personal power is always there, a part of us, ready to re-activate our feel-good experience of life and help us cope with everyday concerns and difficulties too. And that simply by taking a positive stance we release it and it flows through our whole being.

Write these reminders somewhere you can look at them often:

- ✓ I have the innate ability to take a positive attitude.
- ✓ Positivity makes behaving constructively straightforward.
- ✓ My positive power is mine to recognize, mine to practise, mine to use to light up my life.

The energy you generate, be it calm or excited, low-key, pleased or passionate, will influence everything you do – work, relationships, lifestyle and leisure. So everything becomes more enjoyable or at the very least, if you're going through a bad patch, more bearable.

There are countless ways of being positive to give your energy a boost and to give your happiness wings to take off again, if you should happen to feel down. Along the way you'll find other ways of your own to incorporate a positive take into your life and the way you are. All are based on the invaluable willingness to invite in a positive attitude.

Adjust your attitude's current default setting

Once you get the hang of taking a positive attitude, you'll see that like many a skill it becomes a matter of habit pleasingly quickly. Remember when you learned to read? At first it was a matter of getting to grips with the alphabet. Then suddenly you found you could string words and, soon after, sentences together and then you no longer had to look at the pictures to get the meaning. For a while you practised reading aloud. And then you found you didn't have to speak as you read – you could read to yourself, silently.

The habit of positive thinking, if you're new to it, is learned in much the same way, only this time you don't have to struggle with a new alphabet and language – you can start now, this moment by saying: 'Yes – I'm going to give this a go. What's to lose?' And then suspend any disbelief and go with the flow, with a willingness to let your mind-set become more positive and enjoy the whole process.

A positive attitude is a marvellous ally to help you through any of life's troubles and trials, with its powerful energy always at your disposal. When life is in neutral gear, positivity reminds you to be glad and enjoy yourself. When all is going really well, it can help lift your happiness to peaks of joy. And positivity is delightfully charismatic in itself – the more you practise it, the more appealing and captivating you'll find it. Someone quipped to me the other day that it's as addictive as chocolate because it makes you feel soooo good. That made me laugh and it's true!

Improve relationships

Isn't it great when you're with easy-going people who get on with one another? It's all about positivity and one of the keys to choosing a positive attitude in our various relationships, personal, social and work, is to have a balanced perspective and clear perception.

Most of us are very good at not seeing clearly. We don't think we or others do well enough. We flare up or sulk at real or imagined slights. We sink into depression or low self-regard when we've messed up or someone seems to imply we have. We can be masters of passive aggression as we pile subtle innuendos on to our loved ones and others, knowing full well we're pressing all their buttons. Just as damagingly we may openly and aggressively fling downright insults at them.

When we've got things out of perspective, whether we're the perpetrators or, in our view, the victims, we're in full-on negative mode, however well we may hide it.

A negative skewed perspective is the biggest single enemy of positive personal power. It can pierce it, squash it and even destroy it in an instant or in a prolonged, equilibrium-destroying attack.

You can turn your life round to a positive perspective right now by deciding you're no longer going to be in thrall to your own or others' negative perspective. Try it out with the following perspective mind-check:

Think of something in your life at the moment that's bringing you down – it could be something trivial or something important. Now ask yourself some questions:

- O Am I being irrational about this?
- O Is someone having a negative impact on me or the situation?
- O Am I winding myself up or allowing them to wind me up?
- O In the great scheme of things, is this really important?
- O In a day, week, month or year will this still seem important?

Think about your answers. Then go on to:

- ✓ Register whether you're getting the problem out of proportion.
- ✓ Step back from it in your mind so you can see it in perspective.
- ✓ Look at it from all viewpoints, each time registering whether it alters your feelings about the situation.
- ✓ Ask yourself which of the viewpoints are most valid or whether a compromise needs to be reached.
- ✓ Now ask yourself: 'What would be a rational and positive way to proceed?'

Now check out how you're feeling. Relieved; better? Good. If you still feel down and/or jittery about the situation that's OK too – a new habit needs practice. Try encouraging the positive feeling by thinking: 'Yes, that's sensible, yes it does feel better now I come to think of it.'

The combination of a clear, comprehensive perspective and a positive attitude is immensely powerful in helping you deal constructively with all kinds of situations. It also clears any feelings of out-of-perspective fear and dread hanging around you as you recognize how capable you are.

Now you're well placed in the middle of the situation with a clear all-round perspective to decide what, if anything, is the best way to handle it. Often simply seeing it in perspective allows you to see that actually nothing needs to be done. It will take its own course irrespective of your involvement, perhaps, or it will settle down most quickly if you stay calmly out of it. Alternatively, if it's clear that action is needed, you can use your centred, balanced position to think through the best course of action.

Be glad to know you have a good, honest perspective on the circumstances. You'll find you feel better for taking an unbiased look at your own place in the situation, and now, by looking at the way forward with a consciously positive approach, you'll also feel confident in the knowledge you are doing your best and handling the situation the best way you know.

Clearly, a positive, well-balanced take on a situation is the key both to taking the first step towards clearing the irrational feeling that so often makes us feel out of sorts or downright miserable, and to using our rational reactions to lead the way to handling it well.

Using perspective in this positive way changes how we view and make sense of events, from the trivia of everyday life to major events. It makes being positive and thinking positively easy and straightforward. And here is the bit that feels extraordinary: it starts the flow of positive energy – your personal power to uplift yourself and others, to behave well and effectively, and to live and love life to the full.

A good sense of perspective also depends on another innate ability we have – clear perception. It comprises insight, awareness and discernment and also, crucially, sensitivity. Just think how we could transform the world if we all practised it. Meanwhile, start with yourself and become skilful at it. So often we'll find ourselves in a situation and instantly react before we've given ourselves a chance to sum it up. It happens all the time in all kinds of circumstances. An example is the following relationship dynamic that a woman I was counselling experienced.

She went round to her boyfriend's for supper. As he greeted her, she sensed a coldness in his manner. She immediately felt worried that it had something to do with her. She tried to win him round by pretending to ignore his increasingly offhand manner but at the same time becoming more and more placating. After he'd made yet another sarcastic remark, something in her snapped. She became silent. He noticed the change in her and immediately started being really nice to her, finally trying to make love to her. She recoiled and decided to confront him with his behaviour saying: 'How can you expect me to feel loving when you've been so horrible!' He said he hadn't – she'd imagined it. She said she was going home and departed, icy cold herself now.

When we talked this through, we thought about how she could have dealt with the situation with a positive attitude, instead of the fear-driven and touchy one she'd automatically assumed. She decided that she could have perceived that his mood might have had nothing to do with her. Then she could have let him work through it without taking the negativity on board. Alternatively she could have asked him gently and empathically what was wrong and if he'd like to talk about it.

Either of these would have helped her avoid her extreme reaction, which she recognized was not so much about his behaviour as the memory it triggered of her ex-partner's volatility.

She later asked him if they could talk about the way they'd pressed each other's buttons. Sadly he refused and they later ended the relationship because of his refusal to talk issues through or get help in dealing with his destructive moods. 'There was no way we could resolve anything,' she said. I'm glad to say that the positive approach she's been developing is welcomed and reciprocated by her new partner. If ever one or both are moody or have a disagreement, they look at why and bring mutual insight, awareness and sensitivity to discerning what's going on, not just in their present interaction, but in the way their past affects it.

It sounds time-consuming and complicated but it really needn't be: it helps to think of it as good housekeeping – a little positive attention whenever it's needed keeps all kinds of relationships a nice place to be. All you have to do is:

- ✓ Again, stand back.
- ✓ Take a wide view of the whole picture.
- ✓ Feel that all your antennae are alert.
- ✓ What do you sense, and see?
- ✓ Review the understanding that these observations give you.

You'll realize there's no need to panic. You've apprehended the scene with your mind, now let your intuition take a hand too and then think positively, asking yourself again: 'Do I need to do or say anything?' Listen in your mind (this only takes an instant) and you'll recognize the appropriate thing to do. Enabled by your positive approach, your mind has an extraordinary ability to grasp situations and help you find the best way to behave.

Perception and perspective go hand in hand to give you confidence and you'll feel your positive energy flowing through you. It may be because of your body language and reactions or it may be that this energy affects others too, but normally you'll find everyone relaxes and the atmosphere stabilizes to a feel-good norm.

To highlight this, I'd like you to turn it round for a moment and think of the last time you were with other people and felt negative and then as a result behaved negatively. You don't necessarily need to have done anything openly negative – perhaps, for instance, you just temporarily retreated from the others by going quiet and to all intents and purposes cutting yourself off. Now think of the chain this set off. They could well have perceived your negativity and felt negative towards you in return. Or maybe they didn't compute their perception and simply felt negative within themselves. So everyone's mood deteriorated and the impression you gave was of someone who didn't want to be with them and probably didn't like them much. As like attracts like, so dislike is a magnet for dislike.

Think how it could have been. What if you'd stayed in positive mode and taken a moment to think of the best way? Sometimes, to be fair, retreat is a positive step, but if so you can stay positive without being invaded by negative defensiveness or suffering – and making others suffer – your passive aggression.

The energy of positivity is strong, fair and sure – not aggressive or wilfully attacking in any way.

It's an on-going process. You are a work-in-progress so don't be downhearted when you find being positive difficult or difficult to remember to be. Practise, practise, practise it and you can be certain that even when it feels as though you're taking one step forward, one or two back, in fact you *are* making progress. Positivity is like that. Give it the tiniest chance to spring into life and empower you and it does.

My father was a fair, thoughtful man and he showed my sister and me how to put ourselves in other people's shoes and look at things from their point of view. Seeing situations from an all-round perspective became second nature and it's this that has helped me in my agony aunt and counselling work as well as in life generally. We can all do it. You can do it. Try it and see how brilliant it feels when you reject reflexive negative impulses, act positively and let your personal power turn a potentially difficult situation around.

Use body language positively

Perspective mind-checks have even more impact when you echo them with your body language. It doesn't matter if this is conscious or spontaneous. As you follow the exercise above, back it up by changing your posture with a shake of your head: drop your shoulders, stand or sit straight – make like you're confident, rational and positive and feeling it inside and out and feel the boost it gives you.

My niece Amy once said to me when we'd gone out for a walk and had gone into a rather negative mode about something happening in the news: 'Aunty Jenny, think of your solar plexus and your autonomous centre.' We looked at each other's posture – we were trudging along looking glum, our shoulders hunched and chins down. Immediately we both straightened up, held our heads high and stepped out. Looking at each other again, we laughed – we looked better and felt good again.

Whenever I remember this it gives me the same uplifting feeling. As I wrote this I shifted in my chair and sat up straight. I thought about my current state – was I feeling positive and keeping a true, clear perspective? As I looked at my suggestions to you, I saw that it is in perspective, it is true and I know it to be so – I see it working all the time in my own life and for everyone who has a positive attitude. The body language helped me embrace my own positive, rational perspective.

A small example, but it works in every aspect of life. Whenever you're feeling a bit down or apathetic, run through the steps above and show your positivity with your body language. It feels good, doesn't it?

Notice, too, the positive effect that centring yourself physically, mentally and emotionally has on others. A wise person who's advised me about physical stance as we centre ourselves is Mark Rashid, the talented horseman and writer. He brought it to my attention on a course he was tutoring. By focusing on your physical centre – your solar plexus just under the lower part of your ribcage – you stabilize and strengthen yourself and increase in confidence. Horses notice it immediately and relax around you, glad that you're behaving like an 'alpha' as it takes the pressure off them to do so. Interestingly, I've since found that many animals, not just horses, notice, like and respect confident, feel-good body language. And it works particularly well with people! (I'll be looking at this again in the section on leadership in Chapter 2).

I know it isn't easy staying positive when life's being a pain one way and another. But actually if you can just remember to switch into positive mode – even for a second – you instantly realize how much easier it is to take the positive viewpoint or route. Over and over again, you'll find this.

Instead of getting swept along with negative feelings the trick is to notice and then observe them for a moment, rather than race along with them. Now I have an image of trying to stop a huge wave! But it isn't like that – you don't need great strength and willpower to do it. The act of noticing what's happening is all it takes to release you from the immediate clutches of a negative reaction. It really is quite extraordinary, in an instant the pressure eases. All you have to do is:

- ✓ Pause – neither panicking nor jumping into action.
- ✓ Sit quietly.
- ✓ Breathe deeply and slowly.
- ✓ Think what positive steps you can take to deal effectively with the situation.
- ✓ Notice and be glad that you immediately feel more positive.
- ✓ Decide on a first step you are able to take now or soon.
- ✓ Relax, knowing you can and will handle the situation well.

Decide whether to be in neutral or active gear

Sometimes, the positive way is to hold still – there's often no need to spring into action and then staying neutral makes sense. This is another of those split-second decisions you can make in any situation. Both can be positive and one or the other will be best for the situation. With a good attitude and clear perspective you'll sense which is best for the circumstances.

One of my biggest lessons in life has been to know when to shut up! My natural impulse in this regard is to jump straight in and talk and advise. But I've learned it can be desperately annoying when people always have a ready opinion and advice and unless asked it's often best to keep quiet. It can be just as annoying when someone has an overactive tendency to try to take charge of the situation.

Often our deepest need is to be listened to, heard and understood in silent empathy.

Of course it's often healthy to exchange views and information and it's great to debate things. It just depends what's going on subliminally and a moment's pause to see what's apt for the particular dynamic between you shows you which way to go – passively or actively supportive, or passively or actively taking the lead.

Using my dad's approach on this again, following the principle: 'You cannot know a man's soul until you walk in his shoes.' Next time you're with someone who seems down don't feel you have to jump in with your thoughts and opinions. Instead:

- ✓ Pause.
- ✓ Be aware of their mood and body language.
- ✓ Listen to what they say.
- ✓ Imagine you are sitting or standing where they are, feeling as they do, seeing the world around them and the situation they are in from their perspective.
- ✓ Take time to let them speak.
- ✓ If they don't, no need to jump in to fill the silence. Silence is a time for sensing and understanding, and in such moments you'll know each other at a deeper level.
- ✓ In your mind or with kind gestures, offer them positivity, warmth and understanding.

And always use your positive attitude when you meet someone:

- ✓ Smile and greet them warmly, and take a moment to sense how they are.
- ✓ You don't have to strive for this in any way. Simply register what you're feeling then put the emotion to one side.
- ✓ You'll automatically and pretty much spontaneously receive an impression of where they're at.
- ✓ Take it in. Chances are it's 100 per cent accurate.

You'll be surprised how illuminating it is and soon you'll be doing it automatically as a matter of course. It saves you from blundering in when people are feeling fragile or over-reacting to their hostility with your own. Instead it helps you ease into situations and connections comfortably. Enjoy the way your positive attitude attracts positivity from those you're in contact with too – all your dealings with others stand to be warmer and altogether more comfortable.

Touch lives with your *joie de vivre*

Thinking and behaving positively is so exciting as we see how it works in our own lives and simultaneously affects those around us.

Of course you're not going to change any extreme apathy or cynicism that others may have overnight or maybe even at all. But you can get them thinking perhaps life is not as dull or dire as they've assumed, or at least scatter a few seeds which may one day grow into food for thought.

Mostly, though, you'll find people are either already enthusiasts about life and positivity or so intrigued by your zest and curiosity that they're inspired to talk and explore thoughts with you. Either way your respective positive energy will fuse and you'll enjoy a great rapport and probably some excellent conversation.

Becoming bored with or jaded about this extraordinarily complex, beautiful world is part of the dulling-down sausage machine of conformity we're pushed through as we grow up. Teachers rarely have time to go off at tangents, as they feel that to get their pupils through exams they have to concentrate on the usually extremely limited curriculum. Parents are busy trying to fit in so many elements of day-to-day life and don't have much time for wonder, curiosity or serendipity either. Teenagers and young people tend to focus only on what's currently in fashion. And at any stage of life we can find the mystery of the world and our fascination with it has faded.

But you can bring it back both for yourself – and for others. Here is a simple, nicely quirky example.

Before I knew him, Walter, a wise friend of mine who has a wealth of knowledge about country life, became fascinated by vapour trails. He loves to talk about his passions, and so would regale all his friends with his latest observations: how many there were just now, which direction they were going, musings about their destinations. The astounding extraordinariness of it intrigued him and, he supposed, everyone else which, mostly, it did.

They too would start watching the sky and remarking on the shining streaks of white or sunset pink. So they had something in common with him and an interesting talking point.

But one day a man was so set in dullness he couldn't see the magic (either of the trails themselves or my friend's childlike appreciation and the way it lit up his meetings with most others). So Walter's enthusiasm annoyed him and he snapped, 'For goodness sake stop going on about it.'

Walter was devastated. Not only did he stop mentioning vapour trails, he stopped looking at the sky.

 I was told this story a while after I got to know him. I'm a great sky-gazer and, like Walter, have always loved watching vapour trails blazing across the heavens. 'Good – a kindred spirit,' I thought and one evening, when there were 12 streaks disappearing into the sunset and over the horizon on their way, I guessed, to America, I popped round to see Walter and pointed them out. He didn't want to look up even, and changed the subject, so negatively conditioned was he by the man's comment. Now, an interesting thing ensued – but this is how positive energy often works. I can't give you a happy ending to the vapour trails story – to this day Walter only grunts and looks at his feet if I wax lyrical about them! But something in my enthusiasm and childlike wonder and curiosity resonated with Walter and pretty soon he began sharing with me other things that intrigued him and then vice versa, and so began a soul-mate friendship bridging the generations. He is an absolute delight – and all it took was positivity to mine a seam of gold that flows between us still.

Develop this 'Wow – look at that!' wonder at amazing things you see around you or read about or watch on television and you too will open a flow of marvel that lights up your life and others'. Like Walter, you'll probably find some other people don't get it. But lots of people will be thrilled to be 'given permission' by your enthusiasm to be enthusiastic themselves and their energy will dance with yours.

Once again, it's all about having a positive attitude and seeing how your energy sparks and flows resonating with others and unlocking their positivity too.

See how often you can do this today. It can be something as everyday as bringing the supermarket check-out person's attention to something you've noticed that's lovely or fun or interesting, or it could be a conversation about something metaphysical with a friend or colleague. The possibilities, like our universe, are unlimited, as is the positive energy that surrounds you when you give it the chance.

The old adage 'learn something new every day' is a great personal booster too. Taking in something interesting or useful keeps our brains active and healthy and flicks the feel-good switch on at the same time.

A friend has just been on a learning curve with a new computer and a new photo-editing system. She hated changing from the computer and picture system she knew and loved, but it was going slower and slower and was very old, so she thought 'Okay, here goes...' The frustration every time she got stuck with the installation and then faced new ways of doing things infuriated her and several times she emailed technical friends for help. But as no one could call round instantly to help her she persevered with each hurdle.

'You know what?' she's just told me, 'Each time I learned how to do something, it felt fantastic – as though I'd climbed Everest! Why does it feel so good?'

We decided it was because she'd in a sense owned the problems and the solutions. 'I thought I'd never dare switch off the old computer which had been my trusty companion for so many years,' she smiled. 'I thought I'd be far too apprehensive and anxious, but I've done it and I'm really enjoying working on the new one. It's so much quicker, just brilliant.'

This *was* a lot to get to grips with, for a non-technical person, but you get the same feeling of satisfaction and even exhilaration when you learn anything new. Our minds thrive on challenge and new knowledge.

Let positivity guide you

I'd like to make it clear that taking a positive attitude is not about putting on a mask or pretending to be happy. Nor is it about covering up sadness or living a lie. It's about looking at things and orienting yourself in a positive direction. The effect is like switching the lights on inside your mind. On a relatively good day, you step into the sunshine. On a not-so-good or really difficult day, positivity is like a beacon of light, helping you find your way through the gloom. Often, in looking for a way to take a positive attitude you begin to feel better and, somehow, positivity arrives as though of its own volition.

You've probably experienced the phenomenon of one moment feeling tired and apathetic, when what you want more than anything is to shut down for a while, and then a friend rings or calls round and says: 'Hey – would you like to do so and so…?' and suddenly you spring into life again and feel on top of the world. One moment you're feeling exhausted and wretched, the next you're raring to go.

This illustrates graphically how your attitude can change in a trice. But the great thing is that you don't actually need a third party to change from negative to positive. You can bring about a sea change yourself. Sometimes all it takes is the decision that you're going to be positive about something. Or you can make use of any number of positive strategies any of which can re-activate your positive energy. You'll find them throughout the book. There are too many by far to take on board all at once – you can try out the ones that appeal as you come to them.

Enjoy small everyday pleasures

Every day is full of opportunities to bask in pleasure but a lot of the time we live life on automatic pilot, pretty much unconscious of our current capacity for contentment and pleasure, which therefore goes unnoticed and inactive.

All it takes to recognize and activate it is your attention. You can start to be aware of all the everyday pleasures by noticing them and developing an actively positive attitude to them. It's a small practice that increases our well-being disproportionately.

Let's look, for instance, at one of life's potential pleasures often ignored. We spend roughly a third of our lives in bed, but most people see it as a necessity rather than a fabulous daily stretch of heaven. Turn this around and let it be a positively pleasurable part of your life with this simple practice of enjoying the present:

o When you get into bed tonight, again tomorrow morning, when you wake up, or at any time in between should you happen to be awake, instead of thinking about this and that, or fretting or trying to go back to sleep, focus expressly on how it feels to be there.
o Register the supreme comfort of the mattress, the feel of the bedclothes, the warmth, the safety.
o Simply enjoy lying there and be full of thankfulness.

Virtually all of us in the west are so fortunate to have simple pleasures like this at our disposal. So how dare we trivialize it and all the many benefits we have? Appreciating them feels good not just for the comfort factor, but because being thankful encourages us to help the rest of the world attain a good standard of living too – but more on this in Chapter 5.

Apart from being nice in themselves, focusing on good experiences helps get our worries and neuroses in perspective and, in giving us some comfort and respite from real troubles, helps us cope with them. Not taking them for granted reminds us of our good fortune and how appreciation leads to thanks – and a feeling of thankfulness.

Life is full of such opportunities for getting minor vexations in perspective as we recognize – and enjoy – life's blessings. Be glad of them all and do what you can to help others recognize and enjoy their own.

Review your personal attitude recipe

Next time you find yourself in a bad mood for no apparent reason, delve around and into it. Chances are it will be an interesting conglomeration of causes. For mood and attitude can be a mixture of several ingredients including hormonal disturbance, genetic predispositions and prejudices caused by previous experiences, but also of-the-moment common sense and reasoning, feelings and thoughts. They all jostle for position to control and be a key player in your viewpoint.

It may seem like it, but they are *not* in control of you and you can always be the chief orchestrator of the way you are and the way you see yourself, others and the world at large. View the components of your attitude and you can address them one by one and as a whole, approving, adjusting or firmly rejecting as necessary. Follow this process:

✓ Notice the negativity of your attitude.
✓ Stand back so that you can get it in perspective.
✓ Clear your mind of blatant prejudices and preconceptions.
✓ Take on board your feelings and thoughts and check out whether they are born of experience and therefore useful.
✓ Then use reason, with all your common sense and intelligence, to assess the situation and the positive way to approach it and behave.

By doing this, you'll prevent a negative attitude from taking hold and encourage instead a positive way of thinking.

This isn't to say that you'll blindly become a yes person in the face of evident cause for caution or the need to say 'No' or to walk (or run!) away.

I love the saying: 'He who remains calm in the face of crisis has obviously failed to see the reality of the situation'!

Caution and fear are for our safety and ignored at our peril. Sometimes saying 'No' is the positive thing to do, and fight or flight can be the most appropriate strategy too. But a positive attitude, in any situation and however it influences your behaviour, releases your personal power, resourcefulness and effectiveness, enabling you to deal with it practically and with all your innate savvy.

Let your energy trigger other people's

It's intriguing how the state of our energy affects other people.

Again, try this out for yourself.

When you walk into a room with others in it – could be just one person or several – consciously notice your prevailing attitude and see and sense how your presence resonates with them. After a few goes at this, you'll soon realize how your current way of being influences the atmosphere in the room and probably attracts a reciprocal response from those around you.

Bounce in happily, like an enthusiastically loving puppy and, unless something awful has happened in their life, they'll be pleased to see you, flattered you're so evidently glad to see them too and generally uplifted by your good mood.

Plod in gloomily or angrily, on the other hand, and sense how apprehension fizzles damply and almost physically palpably from them.

Try it too, next time you go to a social gathering. Here it isn't so much that you'll have such a direct effect on others and the atmosphere, but rather that the attitude you go in with will highly influence your experience of the gathering or party.

I'm a mixture of introvert and extrovert, but when faced with a large group of people my bias is to the former. I used to dread going to parties and having to make small talk. I persuaded myself that, if I didn't know anyone there well, no one would want to talk to me. Then, a few years ago, I happened to go to a big evening birthday party with my sister, and I was fascinated to see, although she knew far fewer people there than I did, how she moved around the room talking to people and how their faces lit up as they absorbed her animation and pleasure at making their acquaintance. I had a nice time too, talking to some good friends who were there. But on reflecting on her social ease and charisma later, I wondered if it was possible to adopt it.

I can't claim to match her captivating social exuberance, but my new social attitude: "Yes I'm going to enjoy meeting new people and there's nothing to be frightened of" continues to transform the events I once feared. I enjoy meeting new people as well as talking to established friends, and whether I drift round on the periphery or am in the thick of the throng, I relax. And, like my wonderful sister, I most of all enjoy seeing how many times I can make someone else feel good about themselves and their overall experience of the gathering.

It's virtually 100 per cent about our outlook. Decide to be outgoing and pleased to meet someone, and they will almost certainly (unless dogged by preconceptions and prejudices) respond to your charm and friendliness. It's hugely rewarding and instead of getting the collywobbles about meeting new people or coming late into a group who are already intermingling, you'll know you're going to have an interesting, good time.

Love your work

Another area that a positive attitude transforms is the workplace.

Any work done with a resentful heart becomes a penance for you and everyone round you. Look at it another way and even the most mundane, boring jobs are satisfying and give all kinds of opportunities for pleasure.

Just think about this: have you ever, at work or at home, had someone do something for you unwillingly and clearly feeling pretty miserable and even resentful? Reflect for a few seconds how that must have felt to them, and how you felt about it.

Now turn that around and imagine another scenario, where the people you work with or ask to do things are enthusiastic and cheerful.

What a difference, isn't it? With the latter attitude, the atmosphere's better, everyone's happier and very likely the job is done better too. Everyone's energy stays high because it naturally flows in a positive environment, and the effect will be felt by everyone else you meet later on in the day.

It makes good sense. Why work as though you're being forced to when by changing your mind-set it can be a good experience?

I realize that many are in jobs whose nature and content isn't in itself inspiring and interesting and maybe it's difficult or even unpleasant. Positive thinking won't transform the work into something pleasurable in itself, but it can make your experience of it a great deal better.

This was brought home to a man I was counselling when he lost the job he'd hated for years. Suddenly, when he no longer had to do the work that was anathema to him, he missed it. 'I can't say the job itself was enjoyable,' he said, 'but I miss the routine and the camaraderie.'

He also realized that he'd derived satisfaction from bringing home a salary and having the status of being employed. We worked hard on rebuilding his battered self-esteem as he tried to find another job but the competition was fierce and the rejection letters kept coming. 'If I find work again,' he told me, 'I will never again moan about it. I know now how precious it is.'

In time he decided to change direction and help others on a freelance basis in whatever way he could. Soon he was employed as much as he needed to be financially and taking on even more jobs because he was so happy to be asked and to be useful. He came back to see me, not because he needed counselling any more, but to update me. 'It's funny,' he said, 'but although much of what I'm doing is in worse conditions than the job I lost, I sail through it and feel so good afterwards too. If only I could have approached my work like this before – I can't tell you what a difference it makes. And people are so nice to me – I've had more praise and thanks in these last few months than ever before and I realize it has a lot to do with my cheerfulness.'

Even if you know that you really do want a change of career or employer, you can still bide your time in your current situation in a positive mood. When you constructively make plans and step-by-positive-step take dreams forward towards reality, as well as making your work and the setting a better place to be, your positive energy will help you find opportunities and take you along the path you're looking for. There's much you can do to encourage this – see Chapter 8.

Transform failure into success

Where would we be if everyone gave up when they failed? So many discoveries and innovations have come into being because their inventors refused to accept it when their ideas didn't work and got straight back to work, thinking and trying out new designs. So many social strategies that work really well have only been honed after countless efforts that didn't. On the personal front, the supposed failure of relationships that break up is often the most positive route possible and paves the way for both people to learn a lot about themselves and how to get on better with future partners.

Any failure can be cathartic, purifying you as it purges unworkable notions and traits. We heal, we learn, we press on, striving to do better. In so doing, we turn failure into success.

So no more burying your head in self-accusation, blame and shame. If you've behaved badly, make amends to atone and then move on, doing your best to avoid the same mistakes and find better ways and success in any endeavour be it to do with your work, leisure or domestic life.

If a project doesn't work out, launch yourself creatively into new ideas, relishing the excitement and vision, and keep bouncing back as often as you need to. Along the way you'll gain insights and fresh ideas, constantly replenishing inspiration and all the time adding to your skills and the vitality of your creativity.

In any mistake or failure, think positively and see the opportunity – there always is one and usually several.

Remember to resist others' negativity

When we're positive, it's interesting how often people bring us their negativity in several ways.

As much as possible, mix with people who lift your spirits. That way you'll be partners in positivity, inspiring each other and enjoying an invigorating rapport. Cherish the company of those whose humour, fun, creativity and inspiration generally resonates with yours. While it's hospitable and kind to give your time and energy to people who are currently or persistently glum, it is emotionally exhausting. Be caring and sympathetic of course, but have the boundary of a time-limit. Like counsellors, doctors and nurses and anyone dealing professionally with people troubled in mind, body or soul, learn not to take their sorrow and anxiety on board. For them as well as yourself, it's positive to protect yourself, as that way, instead of burning out and avoiding them, you'll have time and energy for them next time they need you.

Others may try to deter you from thinking and living positively as they see it as deluded psychobabble. Others switch off from it because they've read one too many books on positivity written from a cognitive therapy standpoint and see it as hard work. It's neither.

Certainly, positivity may seem magical or heaven-sent because it transforms your life. But it's a fact that it feels good and improves our experience of life hugely.

Positivity has a transformative energy which I experience working in my own life all the time. I'm confident that scientists will 'discover' the effect of being positive and explain exactly how it works in all good time.

And then, as positivity becomes your regular way of life, there may be one or two who miss being able to wallow in negativity with you. It's a bit like giving up smoking – someone who much enjoyed having a cigarette with her friend may quite resent the fact she no longer smokes! Your positive outlook and energy may also make them question their negativity. Just remember that the door to the happiness and fun of positivity is open for them too.

Another thing that people may tell you is that positivity is dangerous, blinding you from reality where negativity is wise if not essential. What they mean is that caution and awareness of the worst possible scenario of a course of action can be effective and essential in protecting you from harm. Absolutely true, but I'd quibble that it's negative to have a cautious attitude. Caution, used properly and not obsessively, is very positive and eminently sensible. When you take a positive attitude it doesn't mean you stop being astute – in fact it encourages you to be and if saying no to things or being wary is sensible, then that's completely positive.

Others point out that negativity is fun – as in the grumpy old men and women television programmes, and when used by sceptical comedians and other entertainers who make us laugh. But whilst an occasional negative laugh is fun, such mirth is transient and can be rather depressing, once the initial giggle has subsided, and it has none of positivity's sheer, feel-good goodness and longer lasting, shining happiness which make it possible to find the kind of joyous humour that lifts the spirits in all kinds of ways.

Travel through life with optimism

A big part of the whole kit'n'kaboodle of a positive attitude is being a glass-half-full person, looking for the good in every person and every situation.

Remember that even in the bleakest of times, like war, goodness shines through the darkness. War correspondent Katie Adie found this so often and wrote about it in her book, *The Kindness of Strangers*. In the vast majority of people, positivity and kindness persist and prevail.

Travel through life, whatever it throws at you, with openness, optimism, hopefulness and your eyes open to the wonder of all the kindness and beauty in our astonishing world. You'll reap the reward of contentment along with a lot of sheer happiness and a liberal sprinkling of joy.

Positivity feels good.

**Two men looked out through prison bars.
One saw mud and one saw stars.**

Be the kind of person who looks for the light in everything and it will light up your life.

Frederick Langbridge

2

Be yourself and like yourself

In this chapter, you'll embrace positivity when you:
- *Know your true identity and like yourself*
- *Work through feelings of fear about being yourself*
- *Realize that you matter*
- *Understand your identity*
- *Register your being, your part in the great scheme of things*
- *Make the choice to connect with your positive energy*
- *Recognize the part your soul plays in positivity*
- *Encourage the confidence of self-knowledge and liking*
- *Become a natural leader*
- *Live life serenely and let go of everyday niggles and worries*
- *Let positivity raise the feel-good factor*
- *Enjoy simplicity and quiet.*

Knowing yourself, being the real you, and liking yourself together foster a sense of internal truth, balance and happiness. Is it egotistic or narcissistic to like yourself? No and No! By accepting the unique nature you were born with and have developed over the years, and staying in close touch with the way you are constantly growing and changing, you enable yourself to mature in harmony with your potential, in love with life. Self-appreciation and encouragement not only feel good, they mean you'll aim to be the best you can be, living up to your promise and purpose. And your aura will radiate out to others, uplifting them too.

When you're true to yourself, everyone around you senses your authenticity and they, like you, relax. When we're aware of our intrinsic energy, potential and abilities, we're confident both inwardly and outwardly. Recognition of your personal power also helps you discover and live your life's meaning and purpose, meeting and making changes willingly along the way.

Know your true identity and like yourself

Not only does being true to yourself and liking yourself feel good, it's also by far the easiest way to live. Many of us spend the early years of our adult life putting on a show and trying to be the person we surmise others want or expect us to be, or who we ourselves feel we should be. It rarely makes for happiness and, because it's a constant effort, it drains our energy. When people complain of tiredness or exhaustion they often discover, as they look into their sense of identity, they are yearning to be authentic and find and live the real meaning of their life. But, scared of doing so, they may continue to struggle to cope within the boundaries they've set for the image they've been portraying.

> *No man can know where he is going unless he knows exactly where he has been and how he arrived at his present place.*
>
> Maya Angelou

Perhaps the discomfort of putting on an act stays nearly dormant, buried deep in their psyche, and only expressed as a niggling yearning to be more real. Perhaps it more openly manifested in recurrent depression or chronic unease. And then there comes a time when a person can't bear it any longer and realizes they have to change and, somehow, find the way forwards to being their true self.

It's a life-transforming transition. Immediately your positive energy starts to flow, uninterrupted. You feel hopeful, inspired, ready to dance and sing with the joy of life.

Understanding your self is a tremendously interesting process. Counselling can be extremely helpful in working out how you've arrived where you are, but you can fathom the past and understand who you are in the present by yourself too. And you don't need to wait for a mid-life (or earlier or later life) crisis to transform yourself. It needn't take years or months or even weeks to inch your way to freeing your soul. You can be yourself from this moment on. You can shine **now**.

It's a transformation that feels miraculous because as you release your inner power your natural energy resurges. You may then, depending on your personality, move hesitantly on the path to free your character and purpose, or bound forwards. Either way, a feeling of pure, child-like wonder and content becomes your new travel companion.

In a way it *is* a miracle that you can enable a catharsis that releases the elemental happiness of being your true self, enchanted with life. And that you can do so over and over, gradually learning the ways that best suit you, and making living positively with full use of your personal power the normal way of life for you.

Work through fears about being yourself

All of us have an image we adopted as we were conditioned to fit in to society – or rather to our parents' and others' ideas of how we should fit in. Although it's essentially easy to change this persona because we yearn to be our natural selves, initially you may find yourself resisting the change. Confusion, avoidance, anger even, are all common symptoms of fear of change. This is a useful way to press on:

- ✓ Acknowledge them, Say, for instance, 'I'm feeling grumpy about finding myself because I fear losing the image I've sheltered behind for so many years.' This recognition releases the build-up of negativity and you'll immediately feel the tension dissolving.
- ✓ You may still feel a bit discombobulated. This is a sign you're feeling vulnerable and that's in a way good. Acknowledging our vulnerability allows us to deal rationally with whatever challenges we face and act bravely and confidently from an informed, stable position.
- ✓ A willingness to recognize your vulnerability is a huge step forward in being authentic. It allows you to express your feelings safely, truly and constructively rather than suppressing them. Suppressed negative feelings can grow and mutate – normal, healthy anger, for instance, turns to rage and/or shame. Dealt with positively the discomfort dissipates and you see the feelings are comfortably controllable.
- ✓ Remind yourself of your desire to be your authentic self and live positively.

✓ Remind yourself of the freedom and joy that being your true self will give you and reach towards it.

✓ Feel the energy of your positivity coursing through you.

Realize that you matter

It's well-nigh impossible to feel upbeat and content with whom you are if you feel powerless. For all the emphasis on celebrity or perhaps because of it, the feeling of being an unimportant part of the world's social network is surprisingly prevalent. Even those who are famous, even those who have thousands of 'e-friends' may have little understanding of who they really are and what they're here for.

Realizing that you matter can feel like a glorious epiphany. And, however 'ordinary' or inept or mediocre you feel, you *do* matter. You are significant, extremely so, and recognizing this is nothing to do with hubris or arrogance – it's about appreciation of your individuality and the effect you have and could have. For you are a piece of the world and all the life and love it's home to.

You do have a say in it. You have a unique impact on it. While most of us won't be major players in politics or other expressly influential roles, we can all contribute. For example, every vote counts in an election and an election can be won by just one vote. Your positive input, however trifling it may seem, contributes to the common good. Every thought you have and every action you take will in some way radiate out and be acknowledged, even if it seems not to have been.

Your contribution makes a difference. Perhaps *the* difference.

Doesn't that make you catch your breath and realize with surprise, if not shock, your influence? So it's vital that we each use our place, our unique niche, to be positively effective and treat our existence with huge respect and great care.

Understand your identity

You may be saying 'But I don't know who I am.' So many people think they haven't a clue. In reality, your essential being does know, very well – it's just that you've ignored it for so long you've lost sight of it. But your meaning, your *raison d'être*, is simply waiting for you to notice, contemplate and act on it.

When you do, the relief will be immense, for as soon as we connect with this all-important facet of ourselves the feeling of depression or yearning or confusion disappears. Light floods into our lives and makes our personal meaning apparent once we look at it openly, honestly and with love for ourselves in our hearts.

Of course it seems the easiest option to meander along in the business or apathy of day-to-day life, resolutely not taking time to focus on what matters most, your authenticity and real purpose. But ignoring your soul's need is damaging and might be literally soul-destroying if you persist in avoiding it. And it is actually far easier to recognize your true self and find the path that's right for you. All it takes is for you to decide you're going to be present in the moment and say: 'I don't want the pain of ignoring myself any longer. I'm ready to face my meaning and be the person I want to be and really am.'

Don't be alarmed. It has nothing to do with shedding valid responsibilities and duties. As you begin to own your truth, so others will begin to adapt. Those who love you can't fail to see your new self-assuredness and genuine contentment and they'll give you scope or encouragement to shine the way you were born to. Others may find it more difficult and perhaps be jealous of both the subtle and obvious changes in your bearing. That is their story and hopefully they too will find the path of life that gives them their own joy, in good time. Holding yourself back wouldn't help them, it would only help preserve their continuing frustration with themselves.

Be yourself – your best self. Be the real, meaningful, often joyous you. Give the beauty of the world and your life within it your full attention. Your life will be more enriched than you can imagine.

Register your part in the great scheme of things

We can be so busy being busy! And many, mistaking solitude for loneliness, studiously avoid it. But everyone who wants to feel in touch with their inner being, their spirit and their own meaning of life, needs some solitude to tap into it. While it's great for personal development to have swathes of time to ourselves, realistically most of us won't be able to organize this on a regular day-to-day basis. But thankfully we can experience the unique joy of mind, body and spirit wholeness in even a few minutes of quiet time snatched amongst the activity of the day.

Now, and in any oasis of time, an instant way to feel this goodness is to do this simple exercise. It lets your energy flow and helps you be present in the moment, connecting with your authentic self.

Wherever you are – it doesn't matter whether you are alone or on a crowded train – experience a physical feeling of connecting with yourself and feeling good.

- ✓ Sit up straight.
- ✓ Stretch out your shoulder and neck muscles.
- ✓ Say to yourself, 'It's good to be me.'
- ✓ No matter what's going on in your life now, in *this* moment really appreciate the gift of life.
- ✓ Now focus your attention on your back, upper arms, shoulders and neck.
- ✓ Feel the energy flowing through them.
- ✓ Smile (broadly, if you like and are on your own, just a little if you're in public!)

This is a simple way to check into a physical and psychological state of authenticity and self-acceptance. It enables your personal power to flow into all areas of your life. Take a few moments to sense it whenever you are feeling jaded, or need an energy boost or self-affirmation and support. It's a great relaxer, too, when you want to rest or play, chill out or meditate.

Connect with your positive energy

If it's so simple to connect with our positive energy, why do we so often neglect to?

Positivity is a choice that's yours for the taking – but you need to choose and take it for yourself in your own hands, heart and mind.

Like any ability it takes application and practice for it to become a habit and a part of your life. When you put it into practice you will see how easy it is and wonder why you haven't connected with it more often. Like most abilities and skills, though, releasing your positive power and enabling it to keep flowing is an on-going choice.

You've made the decision to read this – so you already know, however deep down, that living positively feels good and you hope that it can be your on-going choice for your way, your life. But it's like so many of those things we love to do but so often inexplicably neglect to or make one excuse after another not to.

Curiously, one of the ways you can keep your general positivity habit flourishing is to refresh or renew an interest in one of your former talents or interests. The enthusiasm you release will flush out underused channels of well-being, clearing the way for your positive energy to flow freely again.

For one client of mine, Anne, a big regret was that she played the piano well but hadn't touched the keyboard for many years. She told me she felt that in failing to keep connected to the musical ability and love of music that were once such an important part of her heart's desire she'd sabotaged her soul.

'What would be the answer?' I asked gently.

'To begin again – but after all this time I don't know if I could…' Her spark of enthusiasm tailed off.

'Can you still play, in your head? Remember the notes, the feel of the keys?' She focused on the question and I saw her hands move as she tried it out in her imagination. Her body language changed – she simultaneously looked more confident and energized.

'Yes! I can – I wouldn't have dared think about it before.'

'The next step?'

She smiled broadly at the challenge. 'To lift the lid and try playing for real.'

But as I nodded warmly she palpably withdrew from the idea again, scared of the challenge she realized she was setting herself.

'What would be do-able for you?' I asked.

She thought, rallied bravely and said: 'I could just try out some scales perhaps…'

'That's good,' I said. 'Take it note by note.'

At our next session she told me she'd avoided the piano until that morning but that once her fingertips were on the keys she enjoyed it much more than she'd anticipated. Her eyes looked bright and happy, her face no longer creased with worry.

We worked out a plan for her to slot a short practice into her daily routine. Whether her growing positivity generally helped her steady progress in regaining her former ability, or whether her piano playing helped her positivity to flow through her life I can't say. Probably a bit of both.

And this is true of all positivity. Give positive thinking a chance to spark neglected interests and passions, and the flow of energy and pleasure you generate will help you be positive in all other areas of your life. Think positively and you'll find yourself picking up abandoned and new hobbies, studies and other aspects of your life.

Most of us have regrets about ignoring or not seeing opportunities to exercise our various aptitudes and abilities, to do the things we'd love to but somehow haven't made time for or which, even when we have had plenty of time, we have still turned away from. And yet those things we love, but don't do, are still a part of us and their neglect fosters a feeling of malaise and missing out.

So, along with taking time at least once a day to register your being, your presence in the moment as above, I'd like you, like Anne, to think of a talent, interest or hobby you love, or used to love, revisit it and take it up again.

To help your awareness try this exercise:

- ✓ Sit down with a sheet of paper in front of you.
- ✓ Imagine you suddenly found out you were nearing the end of your life.
- ✓ List three interests, hobbies or activities you wish you'd done more of and deeply regret neglecting
- ✓ Let the realization of them sink in.

You'll probably find, as most people do, you're extremely surprised by the emotion you feel. The other reaction is to realize how easy it would be to bring them back into your life, now, in a very real, pleasurable way.

Just a note, at this point, in case what springs to mind is a sporting or otherwise very physical activity and you feel you're too old now. Increasing years make no difference; you may no longer feel you can participate physically, but there will be other ways to re-activate your interest. For instance you could join an associated club or teach or mentor others.

The thing is to let this exercise inspire you into enabling your interest and enthusiasm to live again – for your enthusiasm about them is a part of your soul.

The first step, as Anne found, is to take your willpower in your hands and decide to give it a go. Step by step, little by little, you walk back into the happiness of your enthusiasms and let their light shine again in your world.

This is a simple way of listening to your soul, and helping yourself back to completeness. As you pay attention to your interests and consciously take pleasure in them, your energy will flow and you'll feel more alive and more fulfilled. Your positive power is like that – it can't help but glow with a warmth and light that transfuses your whole being.

'What if I've no inclination to revisit any of my neglected interests or have never really had any?'

If this is your question, you're not alone – many people have been so involved with their studies and various activities at school and their work and social life ever since, they've never explored the possibility of finding other interests that really sing to them. Others may have only half-heartedly gone along with activities because they were expected to or thought they should.

If this is you, then you have such a wonderful source of joy to explore! We are incredibly lucky today in the diversity of opportunities available to us. Exploring them is easiest online and if you don't have access to the internet at home, you can visit the computer room at the library or community centre in your nearest large town where they are usually glad to help you get started. There are any number of courses to research and most providers will send you information packs or brochures.

It's all part of the absorbing process of finding out who you are, for your interests and passions are a big part of you and your well-being.

We'll be looking at this further in the next chapter, exploring your possibilities including interests you already know you have but don't do much about, and wishes and dreams of new directions.

Recognize the part your soul plays in positivity

Meanwhile you're already getting used to the feeling that your soul is a part of you.

Soul is the flame of life and vitality. It's our elemental source, our being, our inner cause, our innocence and our wisdom.

Although it's always with you, it's up to you and your mind to acknowledge its presence, make contact, listen and in a sense knowingly and lovingly walk hand in hand with it.

When you do, you walk through life in harmony with yourself and know the bliss of self-understanding that is your soul's innate gift.

Put your ear down close to your soul and listen hard.

Anne Sexton

Knowing yourself is about listening and it's as important to listen in communication with your soul as it is when you're talking with others – it's an essential component of understanding. Your soul knows everything about you, your place in this world and your potential and is here to help you, hold you safe and cherish you. If you ignored it or denied its existence it wouldn't disappear – it can't, it's a part of you – but you'd be turning your back on a conscious partnership that's inestimably precious in nurturing the self-knowledge and love at the heart of your positivity.

When all are in tandem positive power hums through you, quietly and gently when you're relaxing, vibrantly and dynamically when things are moving fast and you need extra oomph. Awareness of the strength of your inner being is also of inestimable value in relationships at work, in leisure time and with loved ones – it's like an invisible shield from others' barbs, and at the same time shines subliminally on those who love and like us, who, whether consciously or not, are uplifted by it.

Is it a special form of energy, different from the kind of energy we get from living healthily, that is, eating well, getting enough rest, etc? Yes it is. Looking after our health is part of our holistic well-being and vital to giving us the energy to get through the day. But the personal power you generate when you are emotionally and spiritually balanced and content has its own dimension – similar, complementary, but very special. When you are at one with yourself, calm and balanced, your personal power naturally recharges continuously and smoothly. This state of being not only feels good, but is extremely good for our psychological health, helping us cope with life's traumas and bereavements as well as enjoying the good parts of life to the full.

Anita, 45, had been through a succession of losses. Her marriage broke up, shortly afterwards her mother fell ill and died, and the same year she moved house. Her way of coping throughout this time was to throw herself into her work to take her mind off it all. Nothing wrong with that in itself – many people find working a useful strategy for coping with bereavement and life changes. But instead of balancing the hard work with rest, Anita carried her pressured activity through into her leisure time too, filling every moment and only resting when she had worn herself out. Each morning when she woke up, her physical energy, renewed, carried her into the next round of busy-ness. She became burnt out emotionally and scared of breaking down completely. Sensibly she saw her doctor, who stabilized the clinical side of the depression and recommended counselling. By the time she came to me she was able to concentrate and keen to find a better way of coping with the loss she was still suffering as well as any future negative life events she might face.

Gradually she looked into the reasons she'd run away from the sadness and worry she'd endured. 'I wouldn't let myself stop for an instant,' she told me. 'I thought that by exhausting myself physically I wouldn't have a chance to think about the things that were going wrong. What I didn't realize was that I was draining myself emotionally too.'

Over the next couple of sessions she sought ways to give herself the extra TLC (tender loving care) we all need when we're facing bereavement or trauma. For it's important that we do face them and feel the sorrow and the other emotions that are often involved too, like anger. The analogy of a wound is a good one; if you run away from grief, shock and loss or try to hide or ignore it, it festers. Only when we acknowledge and understand the depth and breadth of our feelings, and allow ourselves to feel them fully, can we begin to heal from the inside out.

Anita got back in touch with her inner self through meditation and with her spirituality through prayer. Learning other simple techniques to help herself relax, she stopped the frenetic activity and began to pace herself. She took plenty of time to be alone and feel her sadness without either burning herself out or becoming clinically depressed. As she recovered and healed, her personal power began to return and she was able to let it work in union with her physical energy so that it wouldn't run away with her again.

She learned a lot: that she could survive loss and sadness even though – or perhaps because – she felt it to the full; that she could heal; and something else that significantly uplifted her, that through suffering she had learned a lot about herself, her inner being and her soul. This and also the love and support of her friends gave her unexpected moments of joy.

Her strength – emotional and physical – returned and soon she was able to fully appreciate the good in life again without being drowned by the sadness.

Encourage the confidence of self-knowledge

The instant effect of the positivity you generate when you appreciate yourself and the meaning of your life is that you'll be more confident generally.

Self-esteem isn't something you have to read whole books to achieve, it's the continuing recognition of your spirit – the unique life force within you that *is* you. It doesn't matter what you look like, though with healthy self-esteem you'll naturally tend your appearance, nor does it matter where your intelligence lies or even what others think of you – self-esteem is about knowing where you are on your path through life now and also understanding that you will find the right way in future. Confidence then walks – sometimes dances! – the path with you.

Confidence is also a natural consequence of being happy in your unique being. Life is a master class in survival you can experience anywhere along the scale between fear and joy. When you know yourself and like yourself, the confidence this engenders allow you to find a natural balance as you develop and mature. We are all learning all the time. There is so much to learn! Be curious, be fascinated, be eager to learn more and more about other human beings, the world and your own progress.

Pause for a moment now, to feel the astonishing universality of life and how the homespun patch you inhabit is connecting, right this instant, to the love of the world.

Be aware that it's so easy not to do this and find great tracts of time have gone by when you've been so immersed in the nitty-gritty of earning a living, bringing up the kids, getting by generally that all you've felt is the worry and sadness of life, the regret for what might have been, the concern for the future. Make time to pause and feel your connection with positivity.

Take time, often, to let yourself feel and in doing so connect with the love all around you – not just of your loved ones, but of the love flowing through the world we inhabit.

Become a natural leader

We can all be leaders, in our own way and in so many ways. A seemingly small positive gesture can have a hugely valuable influence. You could, for example, be the first to say something nice about someone, or to spot their good side and encourage it, all of which will lead to more good, or the first to point out the potential for something good. Leading the way in positivity feels good and as your positive power flows it will have a beneficial effect on those around you and the situation.

You can choose to direct your energy to a project and be curious about and open to any change for the good; you can choose to communicate warmly and clearly, to be passionate as well as compassionate, firing others up with your inspiration. You can choose to trust that good will triumph over evil and to help it do so. And you can choose to support the growing universal attitude that expects positivity and mutual support in business and politics rather than a dog-eat-dog ethos. You can choose to encourage and join the drive for us all to work together to save our species, other forms of life and the world. In all these ways and so many more we can all be leaders and team members.

The poise that comes from knowing yourself and making a meaningful connection with your soul and the world that, together, you are a part of, will be expressed in everything you do. It'll show clearly in your body language and you'll notice how others' reaction to you changes as they become aware of it. Look out for the way that, sensing your self-respect and confidence, they will respect you more deeply and be more inclined to listen to you and follow your lead in all kinds of things.

I stress that you don't need to learn complicated techniques to make this work, though it can be great fun and good practice to go on a course. All it needs is to centre yourself, remember your innate strength, be yourself and walk tall and confidently, believing in yourself and your calm collectedness.

And it isn't only fellow humans who are beneficially affected by confidence. Animals too feel safer with someone who is confident and will see you as a natural leader who they willingly follow.

The effect that this confidence has on our fellow beings was demonstrated dramatically at a course combining horse whispering and leadership skills in California I attended tutored by two accomplished natural horsemen, Linda Kohanov and Lisa Walters. They wanted to test whether a horse's behaviour would react to and respect a positive change in mindset and body language. Three of us went into the arena with a beautiful, spirited horse. We were instructed to walk around as a group with one of us in front leading the other two. We took turns in being the one in front. We weren't sure what we were doing and it showed in our posture and 'herd' formation. The horse watched our progress initially, but quickly lost interest and ignored us as she went back to concentrating on the horses she could see in a nearby enclosure.

Lisa called us back and asked us to resume walking through the arena, but this time with the front person adjusting her body language to portray herself as the strong, confident leader of the herd. We each took a turn in this position. The result was radical, whichever one of us was the leader. In each case, our body language noticeably changed and interestingly the other two people's body language also changed. It was clear they were following more willingly and looked alert and happy. But what took our breath away was the horse's reaction. At first she was as uninterested as before, barely bothering to look at us before she resumed her conversation with her equine friends. But as we walked around, she suddenly took notice of our new focused group and without hesitation, as we passed her, fell into step alongside the two followers, just behind the leader.

The process of 'join up' where you demonstrate to the horse that she is safe with you and then have the pleasure of her coming to you in complete trust is similar and we were all well used to it. But this was different in that we had paid no attention to the mare at all. In this case our personal and team body language appeared to trigger her instinct that we were a herd with a good leader and she chose to join us.

Since that day if I'm in a situation where no one else wants to take the lead, and chaos, apathy or muddle threaten, I remember what we learned that magical day in the US, spruce up my mind-set and body language to that of a confident leader and see the group collectively become calm and collected, moving forwards happily with me as they consciously or subconsciously observe the leadership being demonstrated.

Think of people in your life now and the teachers at school who have naturally inspired your confidence and respect and whom you have been happy to be guided by and keen to learn from. Remember their aura, bearing and demeanour. Reflect on how their body language clearly expressed their ability. Adopt their leadership persona and you will inspire the same confidence – and not just in others but in yourself.

Inner balance helps in other interactive ways too. When you know yourself well and set out to be the best, liking yourself and living up to your potential, you will develop a strong trust in yourself. Others pick up on this and feel comfortable in your company: they intuit that you are safe to be around and will respect them as you clearly respect yourself.

Lou came to me for counselling because she had a pervasive and increasing discomfort with herself and the way she felt with others. We worked on her inner knowledge and confidence in being true to herself. A few weeks after the last of her sessions she wrote to me:

'As I told you, people used to be slightly edgy with me. At work mostly but often at other times too. I thought it was them – that they had issues of their own or just didn't like me, and apart from one or two friends who seemed to understand and get on with me, I shied away from people and social situations.

'To be honest I didn't know if they were the awkward ones or I was – I probably thought we all were! But since you've helped me acknowledge and accept my inner self, and really get to know who I am, I'm getting on so much better with other people. We laugh more together and they don't just tolerate my presence in their lives, they often seek me out. I feel as though I've become a nicer person. You'd say I always was, but didn't know it – and perhaps that's true!

'Anyway, I wanted to tell you that I like myself a whole lot better, and others do too. I know I need to keep going with this self-acceptance stuff, as it's easy to slip back into thinking I'm not worth much. But I'm determined to keep going and it makes me feel very good. I don't just feel more at home in my own skin – I feel comfortable with others too.'

When Lou first came to me she herself appeared 'edgy'. It's quite scary to meet your counsellor for the first time and I put it down to this, but after a while as she relaxed with me, I could still sense a habitual wariness.

Frightened that she would sink into the kind of chronic depression she saw others suffer, she was eager to find out more about herself so that she could discover the reasons for her discomfort in company. The knowledge she gained no doubt worked in partnership with the confidence-building cognitive behaviour techniques she tried, but the change in her aura and body language was evident as soon as she started to accept herself and set out on the quest to learn more about herself. I saw her charm and confidence grow like a bud unfolding and flowering.

Let go of everyday niggles and worries

A part of the confidence of living positively is the serenity that naturally accompanies it. Reflect on those times when you've felt confident and self-assured and you'll see that you also felt calm, unfazed and centred. You looked out at the world from a stable base and dealt constructively with fears and challenges.

One of the most effective ways to restore and maintain this Zen-like calm is to meditate, and I'll give advice on this in Chapter 5. But a simple way to restore and adopt it is to imagine anxiety falling away from you as you let go of it.

We all have stresses and strains, niggling doubts and worries; they are part of the human condition in this busy new century. But philosophers from Socrates to Jung have been writing about them for centuries so it isn't just modern life that's the culprit. And for centuries the remedy for replacing them with delicious serenity has been known – to let go of them at will, dropping them out of your mind so that you can relax.

In the daytime it's particularly simple to do this:

- ✓ Tell yourself to let go of the negativity that's sabotaging your inner peace.
- ✓ Breathe slowly and deeply.
- ✓ Relax any tense muscles.
- ✓ Confirm to yourself the sense of letting go of tension.
- ✓ Positively and constructively address any problems that need attention, or know that you will do so later.
- ✓ Turn your mind to other things.
- ✓ Feel calm spread through and around your body and mind.
- ✓ Be glad to know that you can relax.

In the middle of the night, or first thing in the morning, it's often not so easy. Worries may circulate at breakneck speed around your brain, which goes into overdrive trying to cope. Of course it can't, and so round and round the scary, disturbing thoughts race, making it impossible to go back to sleep or enjoy the elemental pleasure of being in bed we looked at in the last chapter.

There is a useful technique that works almost instantly and extremely effectively in stopping the race in its tracks. I read about it many years ago, and store it in my 'cupboard of remedies' for those times when troubles beset me.

- o Imagine the niggling thoughts you can't block out as little creatures. (Giving them an image makes it easy for your brain to control and deal with them.)
- o Now imagine you are scooping up the whole bunch of them in your hands.
- o By the side of your bed is a pot (imaginary again) with a securely fitting lid.
- o Into it you drop the wriggling, niggling little varmints and they fall to the bottom.
- o Now put the lid on the pot and fasten it firmly.
- o Now you'll find they are effectively dismissed from your mind.
- o Turn over and think of nice things as you drift off to sleep.

It may sound childish and you may feel self-conscious the first time you try it out and it's hardly profound psychology. But it works. Another useful technique that many use is to keep a notebook by the bed. When any worries prevent you from sleeping, jot them down and decide you will deal with them constructively in the morning and not think about them any more at the moment. Again your mind, cleared, will relax and you'll be free to sleep.

The feel-good factor

Knowledge of oneself and one's personal power isn't just a life-saver for people with anxiety or who are hovering on the brink of depression, though.

The quest to switch all the lights on in our life and appreciate it to the full – just as we thought we would – is an awesomely good road for everyone who feels they're not quite where they should be, or that there's more to life than they're experiencing – more happiness, more wonder, more fulfilment. More meaning...

It would be such a waste to go right through life without ever quite getting round to finding your meaning and happiness both in fulfilment and en route. And we are always en route if we allow ourselves to be. We can retain our curiosity and verve through all life's stages and right through old age. With encouragement and our personal power flowing freely this zest for life will withstand life's downside, including illness and pain.

A dear friend of mine, David Morgan, was a wonderful example of this. He recently died after a long, painful illness but to the end he stayed cheerful. His success in enjoying life was partly because of his refusal to let the illness bring him down mentally as well as physically, but also because he continued to focus on others and do all he could to brighten *their* day. Some might have thought he'd lived a charmed life because he was such a contented man. He had always enjoyed his work – he had two careers – whether or not it was demanding, and loved his active retirement too. He appeared not to have had much go wrong in his life. But in fact like most of us he had experienced loss and grief, and he had a number of regrets too. He had faced them all as he did his ill health – with courage, dignity and a gentle determination to enjoy life. His self-generated personal power kept him shining with inner contentment and joy in life and his loved ones, as long as he lived. And all the while he kept learning – taking a keen interest in his own and others' opinions as well as thoughts on the meaning of life. If there is an afterlife, he'll be shining still – a beacon of faith, love and joy to light the way for others.

Enjoy simplicity and quiet

Simplicity and peacefulness help us to seek out the most profound truth about ourselves and the meaning of life.

The wonder and the mystery may unfold in swathes of grandeur – in a stunning cathedral, for instance, or when looking at a time-honoured great artwork. But often it's the humbler shafts of grace that illuminate understanding, awaken delight and moments of joy and lift us forward along life's path.

Nature's beauty and all kinds of small blessings are a benediction for the soul. They replenish our energy reserves and lift our spirits. And then we dance in celebration as well as continuing our contemplation.

Watch out for such moments and appreciate them to the full. It only takes a moment to live the experience and let the joy flow through you.

Love the simple things, the simple minds and the shafts of simple or profound understanding that often speak to us from them if only we give ourselves the time and space to listen with our hearts.

Life is not measured by the number of breaths we take, but by the moments that take our breath away.

George Carlin

I remember listening to a radio interview with an eminent scientist who'd made a discovery that shook the scientific world. She explained that she hadn't studied science at school and college but one day she was out for a walk when she had a revelatory idea. She saw the truth of it in that astonishing flash of insight, but she had no tools – no scientific knowledge or language to explore and record it. So she began studying science and continued until she had the necessary learning she needed to finish and publish her research. Just think what original thoughts we might come up with if we more often allowed ourselves the space to think, to feel, to listen to our inner wisdom and perhaps, who knows, to tune in to another dimension, another stream of consciousness as yet unmeasured and undocumented.

When you know how to follow your own individual path happily and with fulfilment – like which simple things give you joy, how to encourage the laughter that lights up your life and to create surroundings that cradle your happiness, and so many other similar keys that we'll come across throughout the rest of the book – moving moments will happen all the time. They may not be huge advances for humankind like the scientist's experience above, but positive awareness and a willingness to quietly ponder are like an art form that resonates with you; they open you up to a fuller consciousness of life and life's potential. And it feels amazing.

Finding yourself and searching simultaneously for the meaning of life is a bit like panning for gold with hope and dreams in your heart. Just as the gold seekers of old discarded the rubble, so you need to be ruthlessly honest and realistic so you can sift out misunderstandings, deceptions and dross. This way you find your truth – and nuggets of golden wisdom.

Step by step simplify your life or, if that's too difficult at your present life stage, create some pockets of quiet and calm where you can feel at one with your inner being and energy.

Awareness and positivity cannot fail to be a feel-good mix. Each supports and inspires the other. Be curious about the complexity of our world and the life within it. Be interested in others' lives. Love life, love yourself, love others. How can you not, when life is so full of love for you?

Think positively, let the resultant energy flow, and faith will grow in the wonder and mystery and joy of life – and of yourself.

3

Your amazing range of abilities

In this chapter, you'll embrace positivity when you:
- *Recognize natural talent and learned skills*
- *Celebrate your creativity*
- *Value process and practice*
- *Appreciate your particular mix of intelligence*
- *Review resources*
- *Contemplate knowledge and wisdom*
- *Approach your activities with zest, your way*
- *Look after your abilities*
- *Make time for the gift of life*
- *Discover the energy that enables and emanates from all these.*

The possibilities for each of us are many and diverse and, for most of us, far wider than we'll ever use.

We're designed and extremely well equipped to deal with the complexity of our lives and you have your own individual mixture of natural abilities. To a large extent you can make of this what you will.

Isn't that amazing?

Positivity brings together all the elements for survival and well-being you were born with and which, in a wonderfully symbiotic process, in turn enhance your personal strength and allow your personality to flourish too.

Your unique talents, abilities and skill set come from a combination of genes, learning and practice. Because the latter two are on-going you could let your present standard stay more or less constant or even slip, or you could choose the path of inspiration, ambition and *joie de vivre* to increase or juggle your abilities and various intelligences to your heart's content.

Recognize natural talent and learned skills

Our positive energy flows when we're being ourselves and a big part of that inner truth and recognition is appreciation of our current and potential abilities.

But how we love to put ourselves down! To say 'I'm no good at x, y or z,' or 'I'm not creative,' or 'I'll never amount to much.' Others, even our loved ones, may undermine our self-esteem too by labelling us by what they think we're *not* good at, or persuading us to focus on things they would like us to excel at, even if they are not really our thing.

If you've experienced this my heart goes out to you. But the good news is that this history of being undermined no longer matters, for from now on your natural positivity will shine through such misconceptions and illuminate the things you *are* good at, *can* be good at and *want* to be good at. It takes very little effort to change 'I'm not very good at xyz' thoughts to 'I can become accomplished at it if I apply myself to it positively.' Or from 'I'm no good at xyz' to 'Perhaps I could give it a try anyway – maybe I might be able to do it if I try.'

So many things are not so much about natural aptitude as a desire to do something coupled with willpower to learn the foundations and then practise. Having a good teacher who understands the way you learn is a huge help too.

With these things in place you'll be pleasantly surprised at how good you can get at things you thought you were mediocre at, and to discover new things you could be good at too.

John thought he was Mr Average – working to survive financially, but not excelling or even particularly enjoying anything about his career or leisure. Those who know him thought the same. At school his reports were always summed up with comments like: 'Could do better' and 'Should try harder.' His teachers knew he had far more ability than he used but were at a loss as to how they could help him to use it. He filled the first years of adult life with things that soaked up his time and gave him some pleasure, like playing computer games or going out drinking with friends; then he met someone and fell in love and soon the demands of the relationship kept him occupied and reasonably fulfilled.

But after a few years his partner became more involved with her work and interests and John found himself with time on his hands and a nagging feeling that he could do something personally worthwhile with the empty hours. But what? The teachers' comments, meant to goad and inspire their pupil to achieve his potential, instead still rang in his ears all these years later as a negative criticism that he was pretty much useless. He came to me as a last resort, hoping I could save him from the slide into boring middle age that he feared.

I gave him a pad of paper and asked him to write down, without thinking about it first, five things he would have liked to be good at if only he could have been and had had the opportunity.

He froze for a few moments, and then nodded and wrote something down, followed by four more and handed me his list:

1 Singing
2 Woodwork
3 Acting
4 Business
5 Fishing

'OK, excellent,' I said. 'Let's look at them one by one. Singing?'

'I can't. Tone deaf – can't sing in tune.' Before I could comment he blurted out, 'And I'm cack-handed at DIY and would be hopelessly self-conscious on a stage. I haven't the first idea how to function in business – I'm not cut out to be an entrepreneur. And I did once have a go at fly-fishing but the line kept ending up in massive tangles. You see – I'm a hopeless task.' He smiled but I could see the sadness that lay behind it.

'Are you,' I asked, 'determined to dig yourself deeper into the pit of despondency and apathy, or will you have a go at suspending disbelief in yourself, just for the next few weeks, and follow the plan you're about to help me make?'

He had to laugh despite himself and he nodded agreement. I conceded that he might not have potential in all of the things on his list, and asked him to choose three to play with. He was intrigued with the idea of 'playing' with them and a look of eagerness passed across his face for the first time. He'd found life a cycle of work that was, if not always hard, relentless.

'If I thought I could play at acting, business and fishing – not in the sense of messing about but rather just enjoying them, then I'd like to try it with acting, business – but goodness knows what business – and fishing.'

'You're on,' I laughed, 'this is as much a challenge for me as it is for you – well almost!'

We talked around each of his choices. For Anne (see Chapter 2) the spur that motivated her was taking a small first step. For John, it was the idea of playing rather than seriously trying and setting himself up for yet another experience of failure.

He joined a small local choir whose leader assured him he could help him learn to stay in key. He of course soon found he actually could sing and he was dead chuffed at the emotional side of singing with a group: 'I always feel great by the end of each session – it's impossible to stay down even if you start off in a really bad mood!' The pleasure he gets from being in a group of people also encouraged him to enquire about joining the local amateur dramatic society. They've given him a part in the chorus of their new production so he may be able to fulfil his dream of acting.

On the business front, he asked if he could help a friend whose skills lay in selling but who was struggling with the organizational side of the company. For the first time in his life he felt useful and capable of helping run a business and he glowed with pride in the light of the gratitude of his friend, who has now asked him to become a partner in the company.

The fishing? That's been a bit harder. John has a type of dyspraxia that hampers his physical co-ordination, and even with the help of a good teacher he still quite often gets the line in knots. But his progress, though slow, has pleased him greatly and he loves being out in the countryside so much that he's persevering. 'The thing is,' he told me, 'I am getting better at it and every now and then I do manage to cast a good fly and when I do the satisfaction is enormous. I'll probably have a heart attack with excitement if I ever actually catch a fish!'

John's ventures in personal development have had an added bonus. The fulfilment they give him has left him far less emotionally dependent on his partner than he used to be, allowing their love to resurge. She no longer feels pressured to spend time with him and when they are together it's because they both want to be and enjoy it. The individual fulfilment of both partners doesn't only enrich them personally, it avoids potentially crippling co-dependence and enriches their relationship too.

For all of us, taking one small step can be the positive key to a new, fulfilling path. By deciding to release inhibitions born of criticism by playing instead of struggling to succeed, you too could harness a current of positive energy that carries you along to previously unexpected joy in expressing your abilities, talents and interests.

Celebrate your creativity

Over and over again I've seen how doing something creative lifts people out of their blues, takes their mind off problems and helps them heal or cope respectively. Studies have shown how opportunities to express their creativity rouse long term hospital patients and prison inmates from apathy and hopelessness. Our innate drive of originality, when allowed to flow, has a positive power of its own that flushes out our whole system. We feel better mentally, emotionally and physically. It helps the natural process of homoeostasis, the body's continual endeavour to find balance.

A friend who is rather down telephoned – coincidentally or perhaps through some deeper synchronicity – as I was writing the above story. She's normally a tremendously active person, but a recent operation and a heavy snowfall meant she was temporarily housebound which wasn't helping her return to full spirits. Before we said goodbye after a long conversation, she asked: 'I don't know what to do with myself now I can't work. For instance – what can I do this afternoon?' Knowing she is a good artist, although she rarely paints nowadays, I immediately suggested she did some painting.

'What would I paint?' she said. 'I've no inspiration whatsoever.' An answer came to my mind quickly, as I knew she enjoys painting greetings cards.

'Would you paint me a birthday card?' I asked. 'Doesn't matter what it is – could be as simple as a completely abstract blob of your favourite colour. When you put the phone down get a piece of paper, some paint or crayons and just do it. I love your work and will be thrilled.'

I hoped it would at least lift her for an hour or two that afternoon. As it turned out she phoned me that evening to say she'd had fun making a card and planned to use the rest of her convalescence making more cards for her family and friends. Painting was a breath of fresh air for her soul, a first step back to positivity as she continued to heal.

The energy of positive thinking and being is so powerful that if only we give it the chance, with some continuing encouragement the flow washes away even the most chronic blues and apathy.

Depression

Depression may make it physiologically impossible to think about or make positive plans and actions. Like Anita in Chapter 2, it's sensible to see your doctor. Even in severe clinical depression, though, when thinking positively is out of the question, simply reading or talking about something positive may penetrate the darkness. Positive energy is so potent a healer that even a flicker of interest could be enough, at the time or when recalled later, to act as a life-line to recovery.

Being creative, when you approach it gladly and with childlike wonder, has an almost intoxicating positivity. When you release your creativity it's a bit like being in love – you feel as though you're walking on air and in tune not just with the medium you're working with, but with the universe.

It's sad that some artists miss out on the joy factor, and instead get caught up in angst that their work is not good enough. But only they can let themselves off the hook of self-criticism and doubt. Our essential creativity isn't something we should judge or criticize for it's a well of liquid gold and such a wonderful blessing. Your creativity can be the day-stream of your life, a fundamental passion and source of endless excitement and pleasure and/or quiet contentment and fulfilment.

You don't need to devote swathes of time or even energy to it. Being aware of your creative flow is enough to tune in to the feel-good factor. It could be anything from a thought that is original, no matter how trifling and fleeting it seems, to a visionary idea for an invention, theory or project. Neither do you have to be an artist as such, for we can express our inborn creativity in myriad ways in all walks of life.

Whenever you are searching for where your own creativity lies or how best to express it, you can get inspiration by taking a look at the way children view the world.

Children use all their senses with vibrant originality. They spot the beauty in things few adults notice. I remember a little girl I was walking with stopping to gaze entranced at a city puddle. If she hadn't drawn my attention to it I wouldn't even have registered it. When I did, it was just a grey puddle and I asked what she was looking at. 'The colours,' she said, 'Is it a rainbow?' I suddenly saw through her eyes the beauty of the hues of the surface oil and the reflection of the sky. She was right and together we felt that beauty resonating. Everywhere we look – in cities and suburbs as well as the countryside – there is beauty or something fascinating just about everywhere. All it takes for us to get the thrill of joy from spotting it is to do so.

Is this creative? Yes absolutely. Your creativity doesn't have to be about something you make – it's also the way you interpret what you see or otherwise sense too. The art of noticing things and paying attention to them is creative in itself and a great source of positivity.

Just try it for yourself today. Pick one of the examples below or choose your own. You could, for instance:

▶ **Look at the sky:** Like Walter in Chapter 1, you might dream stories about the people in the planes that leave the beautiful vapour trails. Or you could contemplate infinity and eternity, or think how you would paint a representational, impressionist or abstract picture of it when you get home. You could imagine you're flying or floating through the clouds, light or colour. Or, as I often do, you could imagine in a glorious sunset far off hills, a shoreline, sea and islands. Note that as well as the sheer unbridled positivity of letting your imagination flow, the act of raising your eyes has the physical effect of releasing feel-good chemicals so it's a double bonus!

- ▶ **Listen to the people around you:** I often notice on trains and buses that many people are impervious to what's going on around them, as they're wearing headphones or constantly sending or receiving text messages. Instead, try listening to the conversations near you. This isn't being nosy – if people choose to talk in public they're aware others will hear. Listen to what they say. Enjoy the funny things you may hear, any kindness, the extraordinary individuality of each person, so audible in their voice. Notice the different tones and nuances. I love to watch people's faces too, but obviously we have to be discreet and take care not to alarm them by staring!

- ▶ **Notice anything interesting in your surroundings:** Like the little girl mentioned above, watch out for beautiful or fascinating things in unexpected places as well as those you would normally spot.

- ▶ **Pretend you're a crime mystery author:** Keep watch for ideas for your next plot. Look out for possible key or minor characters. Think how you'd direct it when it's being filmed, what would make a particularly good set, etc. Fill in with as many details as you like; the more there are the more you'll expand your creativity. Feel the buzz of excitement of the story in mind and your creative genius. For though you're not (probably – but who knows?) going to actually write the novel, the creative genius within will love the chance to stretch its legs – and shine!

- ▶ **Enjoy the arts and let them move you:** Both the visual and the aural arts are a gateway to understanding and, often, a very special kind of bliss. Revel in the art and music you love and feel the emotions and senses it arouses in you. Feel the profoundness of any sorrow or joy to which they move you. Take time to appreciate them, for they will light up your life and your innate creativity, as all the art forms can be routes for ideas, thoughts and positive energy to come to you. They also may give you a wonderful sense that you are somehow transcending the limits of this world and reaching out to or connecting with a spiritual or metaphysical dimension.

Above all, maintain an attitude of curiosity. Be *intrigued* with what's going on around you. Being observant and being interested in the world is a constant feed for your creativity – and at the same time generates waves of positive energy. It enlivens and lights up even the most seemingly ordinary of days as you see that in fact each day – each moment – is extraordinary.

Being creative is a way of life that we can all adopt and enjoy. Contrary to usual belief, it's not about achievement and making a product you're proud of – it's about living and feeling creatively. It's joyous and it's one of the most certain ways of releasing your positive power and feeling in flow.

Value process and practice

Positivity about your abilities is about the enjoyment and satisfaction of practice and persistence. As described in the section above, it's more about process than product. If you have the kind of personality that desires perfection and expertise let that inspire, not hinder, your creative flow. Too many people are daunted, especially at the beginning or end of a creative process, when their work isn't as brilliant as they'd hoped. The effort to create something you or others will love could also make you self-conscious about letting your personality come into your work.

But as long as you guard against being so driven by the search for excellence that it puts a stranglehold on your natural positivity and creativity, practising is a wonderful way to progress your abilities, honing skills and growing your knowledge base at the same time. The positivity you feel as you do so has a momentum of its own and it's exciting and fulfilling to keep developing and improving.

It's also good to bear in mind that while the saying 'practice makes perfect' can be true, it's only so if you're practising something the right way, incorporating lessons learned in the process. If we keep doing something the same way, we may become more fluent at it and a lot quicker, but our performance is not in itself going to improve.

It all depends what you want out of an ability or interest. If you love it just as it is, it's perfectly positive to practise it the same way. If you want to up the ante, then practice needs to be in tandem with development.

What matters most, either way, is that you do practise. As we've seen before, it's all too easy to let an interest lapse. Keep it vital and vibrant with your care and attention and whether you enjoy the status quo of your knowledge and skill as it is or love the added adrenalin charge that comes from developing it, you'll keep positive energy flowing through you. It feels really good.

So does doing something well – whether it's an everyday task, or an inspired project. It doesn't matter if no one notices, nice though attention is. What matters most is that you will feel good when you give it your best.

> *Even though there are those who might not appreciate a job well done, that doesn't mean the job doesn't deserve to be done well.*
>
> Mark Rashid

Appreciate your particular mix of intelligence

Knowing who we truly are; taking a positive attitude; using our abilities: all are part of our over-all self-esteem and all depend on our intelligence.

It helps hugely if we realize just how intelligent we are and have a good understanding of where our intelligence lies.

In 1983 Howard Gardner posited the theory that there are eight types of intelligence: linguistic, logical/mathematical, bodily-kinaesthetic, musical, interpersonal, intrapersonal, nature-loving, and existential. Ever since then psychologists and psychotherapists have been arguing about it!

I was unaware of his theory until recently, but have for a long time been aware that there are many kinds of human intelligence and that we each display them in varying amounts. The list I'd made of intelligence types matched his with the addition of two extra ones: artistic and nurturing abilities. And now, to bring it right up to date, I would add intelligence about positivity. We all have it, and probably in equal measure originally, but life steers us towards a more or less positive or negative approach to life. However, we can all muster this essential intelligence and revitalize it, so that it regains its original sparkling positive form. Then it is a catalyst for the other sorts of intelligence, helping us develop and use them.

All types of intelligence can be increased too, if we are prepared to apply ourselves, so if you have always longed to be more intelligent in one particular way, a positive attitude with the necessary learning and effort could bring your dream about.

All intelligence types are valid and precious in their own right though, and an alternative approach is to be glad for the mix of intelligence types you have accumulated and polished and practise them in your own way, not concerning yourself with the sorts of intelligence that aren't so 'you'.

Either way, it's fascinating to assess your blend of intelligences and you will probably find that recognizing and reflecting on it is extraordinarily inspiring and pleasing. Our society and education system tends to value academic intelligence more than any other, closely followed by sporting and artistic ability. The intelligences that cover human skills like kindness, empathy, sensitivity, intuition, love and interaction with animals are those that humankind relies on for much of its happiness and general well-being, yet they are rarely considered as very real and just as important as the more conventionally appreciated ones. Of course, they are.

Take a look, now, at the list below to discover or confirm your individual intelligence traits. You'll find that even in those categories which you don't think are yours, there may be one or more particular things that you enjoy and/or are good at.

Tick those that most apply to you and shine with pride:

SPATIAL

- ▶ You can accurately estimate the size and volume of spaces, room measurements etc.
- ▶ You can visualise spatially: for instance if you are altering a room in a house, you can see in your mind how it will look once finished.
- ▶ You can easily imagine how architectural plans apply to the actual building.
- ▶ You can visualise something described verbally or in writing easily.
- ▶ You are good at visual puzzles.

LINGUISTIC

- ▶ You love words and your language.
- ▶ You are good at learning other languages.

- You enjoy reading.
- You enjoy writing.
- You enjoy telling stories.
- You can memorise words – e.g. poems.
- You learn easily from words – i.e. through reading, listening to a teacher, or discussion.
- You enjoy crossword puzzles or games like Scrabble and Articulate.

LOGICAL–MATHEMATICAL

- You find it easy to think logically.
- You can pick out the main points or principles of something, for instance a report.
- You can confidently summarise lengthy texts.
- You can spot patterns and codes.
- You love numbers and mental arithmetic.
- You enjoy mathematics and using IT.
- You have good reasoning and debating skills.
- You enjoy one or more of the sciences, especially the research aspect

BODILY–KINAESTHETIC

- You have good co-ordination skills.
- You are graceful.
- You enjoy dancing.
- You enjoy working out at the gym.
- You enjoy participating in sport.
- You enjoy working with your hands.
- You enjoy intricate DIY or craftwork.
- You have a good sense of timing.
- You measure distances well, for instance when catching a ball.
- You enjoy seeing and efficiently reaching towards the goal in sport and any other physical activity.
- You enjoy training to improve and take as far as possible toward perfection any of the above skills.
- You are good at the physical side of acting or performing.
- You are good at building and making things – and you excel at putting together flat-pack furniture, etc.
- You learn best by doing something for yourself physically rather than from listening or reading about it.

MUSICAL

▶ You love music.
▶ You're sensitive to sounds, tones and rhythms.
▶ You're aware of pitch and metre.
▶ You love singing.
▶ You play an instrument.
▶ You enjoy composing music.
▶ You are moved by a melody that resonates with you.

ARTISTIC

▶ You enjoy looking at paintings, sculpture or other art.
▶ You see pictures in all kinds of areas – the clouds, a textured wall, the carpet, swirls of snow or ice, etc.
▶ You love colour.
▶ You are an artist in some form.
▶ You love craftwork.
▶ You like making something beautiful.
▶ You love homemaking and creating attractive, comfortable surroundings.
▶ You love textiles.
▶ You express your emotions through art.
▶ You enjoy presenting food beautifully.

INTERACTIVE

▶ You get on well with people.
▶ In general you like people.
▶ You understand what makes others tick.
▶ You're often empathic.
▶ You're at ease showing your emotions and when others are openly emotional too
▶ You're a good communicator.
▶ You like company.
▶ You enjoy socializing.
▶ You love conversation.
▶ You enjoy working with others.
▶ You're a good leader.
▶ You're a good team member.

SELF-UNDERSTANDING

▶ You are good at looking into and understanding yourself.
▶ You enjoy mulling over feelings, thoughts and reflections.
▶ You are in tune with your emotions and feel deeply.
▶ You're aware of your good points and weaknesses.
▶ You're aware of your emotional reactions and responses and can often predict them.
▶ You know how special you are – you understand and feel your uniqueness.
▶ You have a deep certainty of your inner strength.
▶ You're a philosopher or very interested in philosophy.
▶ You love to set the world to rights with friends.
▶ You're fascinated by psychology.

Thought is great and swift and free, the light of the world, and the chief glory of man.

Bertrand Russell

NATURE-LOVING

▶ You feel comfortably at home in your environment.
▶ You love the countryside and wildlife.
▶ You like gardening.
▶ You're passionate about looking after our planet.
▶ You're fascinated with astronomy.
▶ You gaze in wonder at the sky and its beauty.
▶ You love the sea – walking beside it, boating on it or swimming in it.

EXISTENTIAL–SPIRITUAL

▶ You're interested in the metaphysical.
▶ You have high extrasensory perception.
▶ You sense there are other dimensions.
▶ You love contemplating or discussing concepts of infinity and eternity.
▶ You are interested in the timeline of your life, our civilization and the world.
▶ You are interested in the spark of life and not afraid to contemplate death.
▶ You are intrigued or heartened by the possibility that the death of your body will not be the end for your soul.

NURTURING

▶ You like and are good at looking after people.
▶ You love animals and caring for them.
▶ You enjoy doing voluntary work.
▶ You are involved with the organization of the local infrastructure.
▶ You enjoy cooking for yourself and others.
▶ You enjoy working for the good of your community.
▶ You are loving and giving.
▶ You enjoy being generous.
▶ You help people, if you can, when you see they are in trouble or need.

POSITIVE

▶ You are generally positive.
▶ You want to build a positive outlook, or increase your existing positivity.
▶ You are usually of a cheerful disposition.
▶ You know how to help yourself clear a bad mood.
▶ You are aware that there's a lot you can do to help yourself cope constructively and emotionally with any situation, however bad.
▶ You feel your innate strength and sense that you can access it at any time.
▶ You have experienced the feeling when your positive energy is flowing.
▶ You love to feel good.
▶ You understand that happiness and well-being are not necessarily 'given' to you but are very much in your own hands to bring in to your life and to welcome and accept.

When you realize and continue to be aware of your range of intelligences, you'll walk taller, feel better about yourself, be nicer to others and help them realize their abilities and reach towards their potential too. Positive energy is like that – it doesn't stop with you, it flows outwards and onwards.

So keep this check-list or copy out the intelligences you've ticked. Look at it every now and then and remember how bright you are in all these ways. Use it to warm yourself by and to boost your confidence now and in the future.

Use it to allay the stress of day-to-day life too. No matter how positive we generally are, from time to time we'll probably find ourselves feeling inadequate in some way, and even those who are confident they're currently doing well in all areas of their life may fear they won't be able to keep it up. This kind of stress is an unwelcome and unnecessary running partner. Time to oust it now and whenever it makes a bid to re-invade you:

- ✓ Make a positive decision that you don't want fear of current or future inadequacy to accompany you any more.
- ✓ Decide, too, that you aren't going to tolerate it.
- ✓ Do this by recognizing your many abilities and particular talents.
- ✓ Live in the light of this: however you or others have labelled your level of intelligence, you have an extraordinary range of ability.

Being aware of your intelligence isn't a matter of hubris any more than liking yourself is. It's about truth and acceptance of ourselves as we are. It's also about humility, strange though that may seem! For how ungrateful would it be *not* to acknowledge and give thanks for the gifts we have been given?

Give thanks, generously. In doing so your positivity will fill to the brim and you'll approach each day confidently and with grace.

Review resources

Communication and support systems have developed and expanded exponentially over the last 20 years. I know there is a downside to this, but on the whole, isn't it useful? And aren't we fortunate to be part of the IT revolution? It's all such a help in being positive about our abilities. Today the internet places information at our fingertips and you can research any area you need to as you seek to develop your abilities. It has created a healthy competitive arena where providers of courses or other fields of learning and information strive for and set ever higher standards of teaching and student care. The opportunities to improve our knowledge and skills are many and so easy to take advantage of.

Above all, it's fun to learn and to develop our intelligence. The quest releases a wonderful flow of positive energy that will help you to supply the effort needed to make the best of the opportunities that call out to you personally.

Positivity doesn't have to be so active on this front though – it may be passive instead.

Sometimes just knowing you have opportunities can be all it takes to recharge the pleasure you take in your life.

Lana told me she knew she should be happy because she'd been lucky enough to find a job in the career she'd chosen and qualified in. But unexpectedly, she wasn't enjoying it and instead had to drag herself into work each day. I asked her if she would change track if she could. Her face lit up as she said she would love to but fell as she went on to say how disappointed her parents would be if she did. Her mother in particular had been delighted in Lana's success in the career she had encouraged her into.

We went through the options for changing course at this stage of her life. We also looked at the risks, which were considerable. I suggested she live in the question for the time being, letting her conscious and subconscious ponder the best way forward.

A few months later we met again. She was still in the same job, but looked and sounded a different person – she was clearly at peace. 'I decided to stay put for the next two years at least and it was really strange. Suddenly I started enjoying my work again and getting on better with my colleagues.'

Lana's decision was based on the fact that she can look forward to relatively early retirement with a good pension, whereas if she had changed course she might not have found work offering the same benefits again. But the feel-good catalyst comprised two strands: knowing she did have a choice and wasn't a prisoner in her job released her from the feeling of its tyranny; and knowing she was staying of her own free will, and loving it now that it was *her* choice to, not her mother's, supported and increased her new feeling of freedom and, in a sense, coming-of-age as a mature woman.

Whether we choose to take opportunities or not, knowing they are out there is in itself a great feeling. Whether we shine inwardly or outwardly it feels good.

Contemplate knowledge and wisdom

Like intelligence, knowledge exists in many guises. There's general knowledge and particular, focused learning. The wise realize that however much we learn, there is always more to learn.

My general knowledge is not good and what I do know I may not recall quickly to order. Understandably I dread being asked to take part in quiz nights or to play Trivial Pursuit! But while I would like to be better at this kind of knowledge, I have a wide knowledge base in lots of things that matter a lot but aren't the stuff of Mastermind. And so do you. Truth, love, kindness, understanding, compassion…

Understanding your individual personality helps let all these things flow. The more you know about the way you personally interact with the world the more likely you are to follow the best path for your special blend of ability, capability and vision.

> *Whatever the circumstances of your life, the understanding of type can make your perceptions clearer, your judgements sounder, and your life closer to your heart's desire.*
>
> Isabel Briggs Myers

Over the decades the Myers-Briggs theory has become the benchmark for human resources managers when recruiting staff. Katherine Cook Briggs and Isabel Briggs Myers' original aim was to make Jung's theory of psychological types understandable to people and useful in their lives. Although I had often heard about the Myers-Briggs theory, I'd never investigated how it could apply to me. I researched it recently as I thought it might be interesting for readers of this book and I came across a website, www.humanmetrics.com, that offers a free test based on the Myers-Briggs and Jung ideas. Based on your choices of yes/no answers to a series of questions, it suggests your combination of the following personality types:

1 Intuitive or sensing
2 Feeling or thinking
3 Perceiving or judging
4 Introvert or extrovert

The test and results are in no way judgemental or critical; no one answer or combination of answers is better than another, nor are any of the personality types – they are simply individual ways of relating to others and our world.

I was intrigued to see how accurate the results of the test and accompanying explanatory articles were for me and others who did the test. Unlike astrology, where we can usually find something applicable to us in all 12 horoscopes, it was, for all of us, extraordinarily apt. We all, too, found it uplifting and, as its creators wished, useful in approaching the next phase of our lives.

I highly recommend doing the test and reading the articles about your type. At the very least, it's fun, interesting and thought-provoking – all very positive – and at most, it could confirm you are on the right way of life that's best for you or, if you're pondering making changes, help you consider a way that's potentially more apt, sympathetic and enjoyable for the next phase of your life.

Approach your activities your way

Are you the kind of person who's up for adventure? You might want to start an exciting new hobby or found a company. If you're into sport you'll be an active participator.

Or are you content to lead a simple life helping others in their business or studies, being a support member rather than leading a team or going it alone and fizzing with the entrepreneurial spirit?

Positivity flows through all of us when we know ourselves and the best way for us to use our abilities.

Something Nigella Lawson said in one of her television programmes on cookery illustrates the different ways we can engage with an activity. She made me chuckle and think 'Good for her' when she exclaimed in her usual exuberant fashion: 'Almost all forms of food shopping give me succour.' Actively engaging with food by cooking might not be your thing, but you might love being involved with it passively, and relishing the thought of eating too as you shop for ingredients.

I adore food shopping too, and wish I could get all my fellow shoppers in the supermarket to adopt this enjoyment. So many people look as though it's the last thing they want to be doing and maybe it is. Just think how the mood of each individual – and the atmosphere in the store – would be transformed if they switched attitude and started being positive about food shopping and actively enjoying it.

The key to being as warmly positive as Nigella is to approach your activities with zest and let yourself love what you're doing. It's a good recipe for living your life.

Look after your abilities

Keeping an open mind is one of the most positive things you can do to let your personal energy flow freely. Only when we are open to life and ideas can we be enquiring, curious and interested. Be enthusiastic about as many things as you can each day. Avoid the negative approaches like sarcasm, cynicism and feigned boredom – they're not cool and can be rather sad and depressing.

> *You must act as though you have no time and your life might end at any moment. That way everything you do will be meaningful.*

David Smith

Positive energy has a momentum of its own. You activate it with a positive thought or action and once in motion it's easy to keep it moving forwards. If you stop it with negative thoughts or words, it takes much more effort to get back into positive mode. When you let this run with your encouragement and pleasure, the habit of being positive is easy to live with and becomes a wonderful companion through life.

Every decade adds layers of experience. In all life's phases it's rewarding and enriching to think back over the years and see how you've developed, how much you've learned, the wisdom you continue to absorb. Never fear ageing. Imagine if the process were reversed and as we aged we shed the knowledge and wisdom, the expertise in our abilities. Instead of worshipping youth, we would long to be able to go back to the wisdom of our previous maturity! Be glad for your ability, expertise and skill. When we appreciate the knowledge and wisdom we've gained we realize how much more there is to learn and it's so exciting. Think, each day, of the chances you have to increase them. Viewed this way ageing is a gift – a fantastic gift bursting with opportunity every precious day.

Your brain is an almost incredibly complex information and understanding system and while science discovers more and more about it, the way it works is still wildly beyond scientific comprehension. Treasure it. Don't damage it with excess recreational drugs, including alcohol, or clog it with trivial or negative information. We'll look more at this aspect of our health in Chapter 6; for now be grateful for the capacity of your brain and look after it appreciatively, positively, carefully and lovingly. Appreciating your intelligence and abilities helps them – and you – to flourish.

Give your memory a hug

The art of memory is not to be able to absorb information better, but instead to get better at experiencing information as a playground for your soul.

Ed Cooke *Remember, Remember: Learn the stuff you never thought you could.*

It feels surprisingly uplifting to use one of our greatest gifts –memory.

I've just spent a wonderful few minutes on www.memrise.com, the website Ed Cooke co-hosts, learning several Chinese words – something I never in a million years thought I'd be able to do, let alone so quickly. Much encouraged, I decided to see if I could brush up my existing French and add some new words to my vocabulary. The amazingly positive thing is that it was fun and made me feel good, so I'm incentivized to practise regularly and really improve my grasp of the beautiful French language.

What with this and the television series *Dream School,* which showed Jamie Oliver's passion for the kind of teaching that inspires young people to learn of their own enthusiasm and volition, I've been thinking of the extraordinary difference it makes if you have a teacher who makes learning fun and easy. It brought back to me how fantastic it feels, as a pupil, to realize you're absorbing knowledge and loving the process – and to realize as well that you're letting your mind play and stretch and enjoy its fitness and scope.

Once we know how good it is to learn new stuff, we're much more likely to study on our own too and find it just as exciting and satisfying.

We were born to learn like sponges – right through our lives. When we use this ability it lights up our minds and the world around us.

Try it out now by learning some new words in your own or another language and memorizing them – let's say three to start with:

- ✓ Choose three words you'd like to learn.
- ✓ Now imagine a picture for each one as a aide-memoire. I like to take in the form of the word itself as it looks on the page as I think about its meaning. Another good way is to think of an association with the word or its syllables and picture it in your mind. If it's funny or a bit mad it's so much easier to remember!
- ✓ Tomorrow morning when you wake up, enjoy seeing if you can 'see' and remember the three words – you probably can but if not that's fine – revisit them and ask your mind to hold them safe for you and it will.

It takes practice to get good at absorbing and retaining knowledge – but it's a very positive process that, the more you enjoy it and practise it, the easier and more enjoyable it becomes.

Another great way to have fun in the playground of your soul is to do that old-fashioned thing, learning by heart:

- ✓ Enjoy choosing a poem you love
- ✓ Learn a verse or three or four lines to start with.
- ✓ Next day, recite it to yourself, revisiting it if you need to practise.
- ✓ Once you've got it firmly in your memory, add a bit more and so on until you've learned the whole thing.

When you recite it to yourself or aloud, don't be daunted by the prospect of remembering all of it – just take the verses or sections one a time.

It is really satisfying to find you can do this, and you add something lovely to the playground of your memory that you can revisit at any time and give to others too.

Learning enjoyably is positivity in action: inviting, beguiling and in the nicest possible way delightfully captivating – for the more we use our memory, the more we *can* use it and the more pleasure it gives us.

Feel the magic and give your memory a hug!

Make time for the gift of life

I've heard it a thousand times: 'I haven't got time to…'

No time, people say, to figure out who they really are and what they'd like to do with their lives. No time to watch out for opportunities. No time to meditate and listen to their souls. No time to do the things they'd like to do. No time to retrain or search for jobs that would fulfil them.

Yet positive energy springs into life when we make time to do the things that are good for us. It isn't selfish. If you are happily discovering the meaning of your life and finding your fulfilment, your energy and spirit will radiate out your happiness to others. Your family, friends, colleagues and everyone you meet will benefit if you have made time to do the things that let your heart and mind sing.

> *The hardest battle you are going to fight is the battle just to be you.*
>
> Leo Buscaglia

Usually this battle is one we fight with ourselves. We may blame our lack of time to do the things we want on our nearest and dearest or on a long working day. But think about it: if you decide to make time for something, you could do it, couldn't you? Be honest with yourself now. Ask yourself how much time you waste:

▶ Watching television programmes you don't particularly like.
▶ Reading stuff that doesn't exhilarate, inform or move you.
▶ Lying awake in bed without enjoying it.
▶ Spending time with people who depress your spirits.
▶ Killing time around the house or at work.
▶ Killing time aimlessly surfing the internet .
▶ Trawling round shops when you don't need anything.

Most of us are would own up to one or more of these as something we do too often even if they're not part of our general life habit. Ditching any one of them would give you the extra time you think you don't have to do something you know you would love to do if only you could. Ditching all of them would give you the time to do all the things you'd like to! Free yourself from the misconception that you can't do the things you'd really like to because you don't have time. Wasted hours are empty of positivity. Don't confuse them with rest and relaxation. Idleness is fine when it feels good, recharges your energy and lets your positivity flow. It's negative and potentially depressing if it leaves you feeling empty and disgruntled. Positivity is knowing the difference and refusing to waste time with the latter.

Just think – and experience – how good your life can be if you control your time and make time.

This is your life to live to the full. Your life to enjoy. Your life to appreciate and cherish every moment.

Energy comes when you release yourself to do things that are good for you and to follow the path that's right for you. When you do, time opens up to accommodate you.

I recommend, with joy in my heart for you, that you keep exploring your options, reviewing your potential, loving your amazingly complex abilities and intelligence. It's part of the experience of being in flow and allows your positive energy to flow too.

We are all learning, all the time. Opening yourself up to this is pleasurable in itself, as your brain loves to be acknowledged and praised and so does your soul, the essence of your character and being.

You have so much potential. Know it, love it, use it – and feel the joy as your positive energy flows.

4

The power of love

In this chapter, you'll embrace positivity when you:
- *Understand the loving contribution you make to the world*
- *Recognize the positive–negative balance of your feelings*
- *Allow love to repair rifts*
- *Keep your faith in positivity*
- *Live lovingly*
- *Live lovably*
- *Live vibrantly*
- *Live joyfully in touch with your spirit and higher power*
- *Appreciate the love all around you.*

Does love make the world go round? Is it all we need?

Love is the greatest positive energy of all. It has the power to protect, save and nurture ourselves and our world. Life holds so much love and the energy of our world is life *and* love. When we sense this and connect joyfully to our own feelings, to others and to the wonder of life in a spirit of love and understanding we add another dimension of beauty and purpose to our lives. This in turn makes us stronger and enables us to love more, enjoy life more.

With love and a positive attitude you are never helpless or hopeless. You have huge power to appreciate yourself, your life, your immediate surroundings and the whole world.

The loving contribution you make to the world

Love comes into everything we do and is our most powerful positive emotion, not just in the way it impacts on our own well-being, but in the way it affects everyone around us, our personal environment and the world beyond. The Sanskrit language has 96 words for love but in English just a handful spring to mind. We call it love, liking, fondness, affection, attraction, adoration, friendship – but there are so many more nuances and elements in each of these and so many other kinds of love – like the love of the world and the world's love for us, so full of goodness, power and joy it takes the breath away. And in them all there is depth and complexity, simplicity and truth and beauty and, above all, positivity. Such energy, such emotion and goodness. And we each of us can enjoy our own mix of love in our own way.

As a child I was part of a wonderful international drive of love that followed the worst war our civilization has ever known. There was a general feeling in Europe and beyond that nations should do everything possible to get on together and connect positively. It was inspiring to be part of the 1960s and 1970s when love was celebrated as the peacemaker that could bring us all together and people all over the world shared in this feeling. We had to face the fact – and still do – that wars continue to be fought around the world. But today the call for peace, communication and goodwill is stronger than ever, the sense of global community growing day by day. Love refuses to be defeated by those who try to deny, negate or sabotage it.

Bring to mind the power of love whenever the cynics and sceptics talk of the inevitable destruction of our civilization and the planet. Let love flow from your heart to mankind right around the world. Join the fight to look after this earth and do not be downhearted.

As you practise being positive, others may accuse you of looking at the world through rose-coloured glasses. And yes, this is in one way a good analogy for positive thinking! But having a positive attitude also means looking and thinking about the real picture clearly, realistically and constructively. The hue is certainly warm, but positivity and love aren't blind; they seek out the goodness there is or can be, however bleak the scene, and they know the difference between fake and true.

Positivity is love and vice versa. If scientists, politicians, philosophers and every single one of us persistently and passionately reach towards the same goal of the peace and long-term future of the world, we will be united in the positive energy of love.

Balance the negative with the positive

Most men lead lives of quiet desperation and go to the grave with the song still in them.

Henry Thoreau

You only have to look at people's faces or hear them grumble on and on about what's wrong with their lives and the world to know how worried, anxious or inexplicably sad some of them feel. How sad that they aren't tuned in to the melody of life that could be theirs and singing their song of joy.

Avoid at all costs getting stuck in such a groove of negativity. If you fear you already have, do whatever it takes to climb out. Whenever you feel yourself slipping back into negative thoughts or speech, stop yourself there and then and consciously switch into positive gear.

Those around you will be surprised at first that you're going against their stream of constantly downwardly oriented conversation. They won't like it because it will make them realize they are being grumpy or mean too.

It's so easy to get into a rut as you think or talk. Of course it's good to let off steam if something annoying or otherwise negative has happened to you or yours. It's healthy to know and show your feelings. What's not good is when you keep repeating the same negative thought, or move to another topic but keep the same negative vibe. Change out of it instantly this way:

- ✓ Notice you are being chronically negative.
- ✓ Stop yourself immediately.
- ✓ Notice your body language.
- ✓ Breathe out the negativity and breathe in positivity.
- ✓ Think how love could change your attitude.
- ✓ Now, with that in mind, say or think something positive.
- ✓ Resist your own or others' prompting to return to negative comments.
- ✓ Note the way you now feel physically and mentally.
- ✓ Feel the relief and pleasure of restoring positive flow.

The way our body language and inner states of being change when we follow the above sequence from negative to positive is fascinating.

Feel how the tension drops away from you, dissolving as it goes. Love the way losing the negativity frees you to get on with other things constructively and pleasurably. Watch the impact your change in attitude has on others too. They'll likely be discomfited at first but will probably soon start to follow your lead.

This happens, too, when you gently but firmly point out to someone that they're being needlessly negative. This happened with me and two friends just recently.

Luke had just been told by another friend of an undeserved negative comment a mutual acquaintance had made about him. He related it to us and said how unfair it was. As he talked he grew irate and his whole body tensed. I was surprised by his reaction as the comment was truly insignificant. But as he started repeating the tale, we saw that this normally affable guy was getting it out of proportion and had not only lost his cool but was in danger of phoning the woman who'd made the false assumption and letting rip at her. We sympathized with his outrage and said something along the lines of: 'Yes it must be really annoying, but hey, in the great scheme of things it's honestly not worth challenging her. We'd tell you if it was. Calm down.'

For a few moments you could see him struggling with this – he was caught up in the negativity of his thoughts. Then his expression softened a little and he said, 'I actually like her – I don't want to fall out with her.' We said, 'Good, there is no need.' I mentioned that people often say catty things they don't really mean to show off or because they're having a negative moment. He visibly relaxed, his shoulders dropping and frown disappearing too. 'You're right,' he said, 'I was getting my knickers in a twist. Sorry folks. Rant over.'

Whenever negative feelings are running away with you and driving you towards a defensively aggressive reaction, it's well worth pausing, just as Luke managed to, and asking yourself: 'Is there a better way of reacting?' Then consider how love could change the situation for the better. Love, although Luke may not have realized, had a big effect on his situation. Love for himself helped him drop the hurt and subsequent fear and anger that was spiralling out of control. It made sense to let it all go. And love helped him remember that he liked the woman too.

Let love repair rifts – and the world

So often people have told me of hurts that have caused them to take such umbrage they've sworn: 'I will never speak to him (or her) again.'

Yet, however adamant they were, nearly always such feuds are in time dissolved. The catalyst is love.

We are emotional creatures and it's natural to experience a full spectrum of emotions. Sometimes we need to let anger out and this can cause major disagreements and even bust-ups. But most of us have deep wells of love within us and in time use it to build bridges and repair damage. The healing power of your love, shining quietly, can also help others get grievances into perspective, deal with them constructively, forgive and get on better together. Often love is strengthened by this reconciliation process.

It helps to remember that usually fear is behind anger and umbrage. By choosing not to ruffle feathers even further but to be a peacemaker, you'll shine love into the corners of the fear giving you understanding of your own and their behaviour. You may find this is all it takes for the disagreement to evaporate; otherwise your new insight will help you constructively manage and soothe it. Love is tender understanding but at the same time it heals and helps us accept change.

Laughter can be your ally here; gentle humour takes the wind out of hurt feelings and helps us see we're over-reacting, and there's nothing like a good laugh to restore our equilibrium.

Another catalyst in solving disputes is to ask yourself what someone you admire for their diplomacy and wisdom would do in the same situation. With my Christian upbringing, it's natural for me to pause and think: 'OK. What would Jesus do here?' Or perhaps I'll think of a fellow agony aunt or uncle whose wisdom I highly respect. Or you could simply ask: 'What would love do?' It gives you an instant clear, positive perspective and a constructive, healing attitude.

We tend to think of love as being primarily involved in couple or family relationships. Certainly, these types of love have great power to restore the equilibrium of good will after a disagreement or fight.

But love goes far beyond romantic, sexual and blood relationships: we all have access to its properties in all aspects of life and it has such power that by letting it into our thoughts and actions not only do we feel good in the moment, it can transform great swathes of negativity into positivity.

A good example is the way philanthropists have proven that we can all have a massive impact on world poverty and in changing the atmosphere between the world's superpowers. Bill Gates and Bob Geldof spring to my mind – they have caused billions of us around the world to sit up and take notice of our responsibility to others, right around the globe. Politicians are increasingly realizing that looking after our planet and all its wildlife is important to each and every one of us and if they want us to vote for them they'd better do something positive about it.

It's taken time to get this zeitgeist going, and it will take more for nations to learn to work together truly efficiently. But it is happening and it started and continues with the power of love behind it.

We don't yet understand the science of love and positivity. But it is clear to me that it is an energy that is there around us and in us all the time. When we ignore it we let negativity flow. When we welcome it and use it generously and joyfully in our lives positivity shines bright.

Keep your faith in positivity

Whether or not we have a religious faith, most of us, if we just stop to think, believe in the power of good over evil but realize how easy it is to let the latter reign. As English philosopher Edmund Burke said, the only thing necessary for the triumph of evil is for good men to do nothing.

Don't be fazed by friends who are apathetic or bored when you're fired up with positivity about world politics or aid, or when they yawn at your enthusiasm for goodness and love and the concept of positive thinking. Their story is not yours so don't fret if you can't get them to see your point of view. Accept that you differ and they have as much right to their opinion as you to yours.

Keep speaking up for goodness and truth and don't ever let yourself be apathetic about and bored with anything you notice around you that's not right. It isn't true that the individual can't make a difference. You can make a difference far greater than you realize. As we saw in Chapter 2, just as you matter, so do your thoughts and actions. You might not see the effect of your life now, or perhaps ever, but if you could you would be astonished at the influence you have had. You don't even have to be an activist to change things positively. A kind word or an understanding insight could completely change someone's life for the better. You can be a catalyst for positivity.

I add just a note here about the need for scepticism and caution, as pointed out to me by a friend. 'Remember how Chamberlain was duped by Hitler, losing us valuable time,' he reminded me chillingly as an example. He's right in that we need to be astute and non-dupable as far as possible and we need to be aware that negativity is powerful too. This is all the more reason for making love and positivity the core ethos of our lives and letting their energy flow in the on-going fight for the freedom and well-being of all people.

They are good and they do feel good and they are strong and sure. No need to defend them – just live in their light and it will automatically shine from you.

Live lovingly

Every time we are spiteful, that negativity goes out into the ether. Who knows what ill it will cause? What we do know is that being unkind has an immediate negative effect on us. It feels nasty inside and shabby, and it perniciously spoils the day.

So stay aware of your emotions and others'. Remember they are human beings with emotions just like yours. You don't know all that's going on in another person's life at the moment, what heartache or fear they are experiencing. So catch any negative thought back and replace it instantly with a kind one or – if you just can't be kind about that person – at least a patient one.

Tot up the moments you've spent during your life feeling frustrated or mean or downright aggressive and you'll see what great chunks of your time you've wasted on that negativity. The brilliant news is that there's no point dwelling on this – from now onwards you can decide to live lovingly, trying to find the best in people and letting love remind you that you don't know the struggles they have in their lives, the frustrations, negative emotions and sadness they're going through, the way they were brought up and the hurts they've suffered.

A visualization I do with people who have a grievance against a parent, for example, is extremely illuminating and healing. It involves sitting quietly and letting yourself imagine your mother, say, as first a younger woman, then a teenager, child and finally as a very small child. At each stage feel deep in your bones and heart how it was to be them. Most weep as they 'experience' (and it is often a powerful experience) the life of the little girl and realize that their mother, like all of us, started out wanting only to love and be loved. How easy, then, it is to forgive them for the way they are now or have been with you in the past. How easy it is, if not to forgive others their negativity and unkindness, at least to understand the trials they've been through, and let a wave of love go out from you to them.

For sure, they may be so armoured against love and positivity that they can't feel it, let alone respond. But one day they may. And meanwhile, your patience, understanding and love will restore your own equilibrium, and also make further interaction with them easier to cope with.

The wonder of living lovingly is that not only can the smallest loving gesture transform someone's life, it automatically transforms yours in that moment and often pleasantly permeates the rest of the day too, usually warming others in the process.

It's become the norm to act when we're out and about in public as though each of us is an island. Apart from social courtesies like standing aside for each other, we scarcely interact at all. Try engaging with others. You might find that one or two them hardly respond at all. But when they do it's as though a light goes on. Smile at people you meet and watch their faces animate as they recognize the message of good will.

On a train, for example, when you're embarking on a journey of any length, say hello to the people you sit down next to or opposite. See if you can open the way for communication – for example you might like to comment on something beautiful or interesting you see through the window or simply ask for information such as whether the train is expected to arrive on time or which direction the buffet car is. This isn't about being annoying, I hasten to add – it's just acknowledging their presence and fellow humanity. Say goodbye when you or they depart too. Remember, your warmth towards them might be the only bright spot of their day – just think how sad it would be if you ignored them, as everyone else had.

Try engaging the attention of people behind tills in shops, the post-offices, and so on, too. See the way they switch on as they realize with surprise that you're actually noticing them as a real person. And register how good you feel about yourself every time you make a connection or even just try to. Being loving, because it's positive, feels good.

An easy everyday way to lovingly give cheer to others when they visit or phone you is to fill your welcome with love in your voice and eyes. When people sound or look as though they are really pleased to hear or see me, it makes my heart give a little jump of pleasure. When you answer the phone with 'Wendy! Hi – how are you?', suffusing your greeting with the feeling you are really thrilled it's them, you'll hear the pleasure in their response too. A simple little thing – but the little positive things like this really do mean a lot.

For the first few years I exhibited work at a local arts and crafts gallery, the owner Alan, always made me feel special. Catching sight of me, even if I arrived unannounced at a busy time, he'd always come over and say 'Jenny! How lovely to see you.' The warmth in the words, his face and body language was so welcoming I always felt a million dollars. Sadly he died a while back. At his funeral everyone speaking of him said exactly the same thing – how welcoming he always was, how pleased he made you feel he was to see you. Everyone loved him, and whether or not he loved us all, the pleasure he had from his welcoming attitude and our gladness to see him in spontaneous response, surely added another element of happiness to his already enthusiastic, inspired life. Today his wife and sons continue his spirit of welcome at the gallery, in their own individual ways continuing the loving atmosphere.

Other kinds of generosity of spirit have the same effect. You don't have to give rich material goods. The most positively loving thing you can give is your thoughtfulness, kindness and time. Before you say 'I'm too busy,' I stress again – it need only take seconds, like the warm welcoming greeting above or a helping hand every now and then. If you're feeling resistant, it may help to think of the beautiful biblical text: 'Be not forgetful to entertain strangers for thereby perhaps you entertain angels instead.'

'Angels' here is translated from Greek and the word also means messengers. Perhaps every one we meet has a message for us that we'll only benefit from if we welcome them and are prepared to willingly give a little of our time.

Loving courtesy costs nothing, could be life-changing for the recipient and is quietly but very positively powerful in its own right.

You can help fill your life with a flow of positivity by making a collection of the instances of kindness and love you notice each day or week. This is a recent list of mine:

- ✓ A whole family on the train home when there was standing room only. I was wedged in between two booths, all eight seats taken by two men and a family of mum, aunt and four daughters, one of whom had quite extreme learning difficulties and though a sweetheart gave them no peace. They were just lovely with her – endlessly patient even though you could see they were tired after a long day and occasionally a bit worried that the people around would get fed up with her noise and jumping about. They were so pleased when the men left the train and I sat down with them – I guess they were used to people avoiding them and sitting as far away as they could. It was clear how much they loved her and their sense of humour was great too – we all smiled and laughed – especially when she sang a pop song at the top of her voice and we all joined in, to her great delight. I was sorry to say goodbye to them all when they got off the train. I wanted to tell them I thought they were all brilliant but thought it might sound patronizing. Anyway – they are and they deserve to win a Nobel prize!
- ✓ The BT engineer who drove all the way back from the town (a 16-mile round trip in freezing, snowy weather) to fix a troublesome connection and rang later to make sure it was still working.
- ✓ My neighbours – at my last house and this one – who phone or pop round to check all is well in bad weather.
- ✓ An American man in Holland Park, London – a total stranger who helped my sister carry her shopping home the other evening. Who said chivalry was dead?

- ✓ ProPrint in Carmarthen, who make the setting and printing of projects so easy. The whole team is not only efficient but unfailingly cheerful and encouraging. A real 'can do' attitude which is so refreshing.
- ✓ The driver of a car I backed into. When I apologized profusely (yes I know you're not supposed to admit guilt in road traffic accidents but this was clearly my fault alone) for the damage I thought I'd caused – a big dent – he said: 'It's OK love, that was already there.' I thanked him for his honesty. 'Well now you can enjoy the rest of the day,' he said with a lovely smile.
- ✓ The butcher in the main street who always greets me cheerfully and gives me a bag of bones for the dog.

Kindness is an aspect of love not often remarked for having energy but it positively hums with it. The nice thing about having a running list of kindnesses is that once in a while, if you're having a 'what's the world got against me' kind of day, you can look back at it to remind yourself of loving behaviour and random acts of kindness you've been on the receiving end of. Make sure you give out too – as my 93-year-old friend Lee says: 'Cast your bread upon the waters and it will come back as ham sandwiches.' She doesn't mean that we give to get, but that in a life of caring for others, making them laugh and generally lighting up the lives of everyone round her, she has seen that life is good when we give out. The current of positivity goes full circle.

Remember:

- ▶ Be aware
- ▶ Have a kind attitude
- ▶ Love

Live lovably

A major catalyst for being lovable is believing in the loving kindness of others. When we do, we have an aura that attracts love in every measure ranging from everyday courtesy from strangers to one-to-one love from our nearest and dearest.

It works the other way too. When I find myself grumbling about a lack of manners, thoughtlessness or unkindness in life today, I wonder if I could have had something to do with it. It could be that

I'm nothing whatsoever to do with it and simply the innocent target of the other person's negative state. But very often, if I take time to look back, I'll remember that I was negative too. An easy way is to think of your aura and remember how it felt when the apparent discourtesy or rudeness happened.

Auras

It's widely believed that an aura is a field of subtle, luminous radiation surrounding a living being. It has a distinctive but intangible quality and has also been described as being like an invisible breath or atmosphere around them.

It can be illuminating when you realize another person's negative behaviour towards you is in reaction, partly or sometimes completely, to the negativity you are harbouring at the time. Negativity is like a magnet for more negativity. It draws it in from others around us, usually completely unconsciously, and mirrors it back.

It's easy to rise to it when others are originating negativity too. As we become aware of it, a defensive-aggressive reaction can, unless we're watchful, erupt.

The answer is to substitute immediately a loving attitude. Think how to defuse the situation. By refusing to bounce their negativity back you give them the chance to adjust to a more positive attitude themselves and calm down or be thoughtful instead.

When you bring love, courtesy and consideration into the equation, it's much easier to think logically. Like the couple in Chapter 1, often you may realize that the negativity of either one or both of you has little to do with your connection in the moment, but has come from a memory of something hurtful from way back in your life or theirs. Often there's no need to analyse this to restore harmony in your present together, just being aware of it is often enough to defuse the negativity and send it back to where it belongs, the past. If your aura or theirs still fizzes with negativity, you can at least detach yourself from it rather than mirroring and thereby exacerbating it.

To be loving and lovable, you don't even have to go around being actively loving all the time. Simply by staying in passive mode and not reacting angrily, as above, and by not being unkind or, however mildly, putting people down or projecting debris from the past on to them, you enable love to be at the heart of your equilibrium.

Try it. Instead of making a derogatory comment – we've all heard people telling their loved ones how stupid they are, for example, or saying hostilely something like 'What's the matter with you?' – think of something nice to say. Instead of negative criticism, make it positive. Instead of being sarcastic, think of something you can praise. Instead of mirroring their negativity with your swiping outrage and over-reaction, don't engage with it. Staying positive inside yourself and, in relation to them, you'll feel your spirit dancing with love instead of seething with emotion and defensiveness or judgement and criticism. The love will circulate round you, round them, round the room. Feel it. Try it for yourself next time you're with someone:

- ✓ Listen to them. Really listen – be aware of their aura and their body language as well as their words.
- ✓ Resist the urge to comment negatively.
- ✓ Refuse to entertain the thought of putting them down in any way.
- ✓ Say something encouraging.
- ✓ Say something else positive.
- ✓ Say something loving.
- ✓ Make a kind gesture (get something for them, offer a cup of tea, whatever).
- ✓ Notice how you're feeling.
- ✓ Feel the power of loving behaviour.
- ✓ Notice if the energy of your positivity has a physical feeling – for instance you might have a warm, tingling feeling across your shoulders.
- ✓ Notice if you've helped the other person shake off any negativity they came in with, and encouraged their positivity to flourish. If not, and they can't let their mood dissolve despite your refusal to reflect it, let them be and take your leave of them courteously, calmly and lovingly, offering to talk the next day.
- ✓ If you are both positive, feel how good the atmosphere in the room is and the connection between you.

As well as being sensitively aware of others and their behaviour, it's about being self-aware too. Notice if any aspect of your behaviour, however much you pretend it's well intentioned, is actually getting back at someone or attacking them surreptitiously. When you know someone's sensitivities, it's very easy to do this, all the while feigning innocence. But causing harm to others inevitably causes harm to yourself as well. Don't go there – it would be as miserable as scoring an own goal. Pause for a moment. Reflect. And instead of the veiled barb, think what you can do or say instead that's truly kind and helpful. Contrast the way you then feel. You'll find it's completely different – warm and pleasant – your whole life will feel so much better. This advice comes from my heart and my personal experience. Whenever I've been sharp, however much I thought they deserved it, however self-righteous or clever it felt in the moment my arrow struck, I've always regretted it. There is always a better way born of awareness, love and positivity. It always works better and gives you the inestimable blessing of inner peace.

Self-awareness and love also guard against the passive aggression of assumed martyrdom. It wasn't until Kim learned a little about emotional intelligence that she realized she'd lived most of her life being a martyr in reaction to what she termed the abuse of her partner and others. She wanted to make out she was an angel for tolerating them. As a result they felt mean but somehow subtly encouraged to continue their attempts to dominate her. As she began to understand that she was exhibiting passive aggression, she learned how to deal constructively with the seething anger she harboured. She found the courage to acknowledge the truth to herself and to speak about it. She also started to accept others the way they were instead of trying to change them. This didn't mean accepting abuse – far from it. As she stopped projecting an aura of victimhood and martyrdom, the pressure of her suppressed hostility dissolved. Suddenly they were with a lovable, warm person. Resistance on both sides disappeared and one-to-one, family and multi-dimensional love was given space to breathe and grow.

'It was very strange,' she explained, 'the way people changed when my attitude shifted. As I began to be the authentic me, I actually didn't have to stand up for myself, I just was the real me and people in general started treating me with respect and love. Thank goodness I gave positivity a chance. I can't believe how good it feels and the way it's transformed our lives.'

So much family and relationship dissonance is pre-empted if we pause, stop negativity forming, and think 'OK, how would love act here?'

Notice as you think this whether it has an instant effect on you physiologically. As I wrote it I found myself taking my hands off the keyboard, leaning back in my chair, stretching and breathing deeply, all signs that I was feeling the energy of positivity and how it relaxes us as it re-energizes us.

Love and positivity are one. They encourage each other, enable each other. They encourage and enable you to be the real, positive, loving and lovable you.

Letting love be our main reason for being is an integrated process. As you become more loving, you'll be more lovable and will love yourself and others more too. All the aspects covered in this chapter and the whole book work together, dovetailing in the positive power of love and life.

Live and love vibrantly

I've never claimed to have the answers to life. I only put out songs and answer questions as honestly as I can...But I still believe in peace, love and understanding.

John Lennon

When we let love infuse our lives it flows through our veins, our hearts. It doesn't mean you're all sweetness and light, all the time – some of the world's shining beacons of love have been the angriest and sometimes very bitter, crusaders! But nevertheless, they – just as we can – let love live vibrantly, passionately, quietly, strongly within their souls and radiate out to others. The love they personify continues to shine even after their death. They were driven by love, as we can be.

When we speak of 'being driven' it suggests a force is at work, pushing them on, powering them and this is very true. The power is positive energy, and in this case the positive energy of love.

Love has such power it energizes those who feel it and express it in their lives. Sometimes they are the quiet ones who go largely unnoticed, unobtrusively spreading good will and, if they have children, carefully bringing them up to be loving, thoughtful people.

Sometimes they are world leaders or inspirers who revolutionize a generation and beyond.

When Bob Geldof was asked why he continued to organize fund raising events for Africa, he answered: 'Because I can.'

However much sadness and badness there is it will never overcome the power of love, for it is inextinguishable. Even in the darkest times, love conquers all. Love heals depression, rises above addiction, helps us every step of the way as we cope with the pressures of life.

Let's not confuse it with the chemically or psychologically induced emotions many think of as love – for instance the in-love or in-lust feelings early in a relationship, the co-dependency of some couples or neediness. Love doesn't seek to control, is not needy, realizes that initial attraction can but does not always transform to a deep, realistic, lasting love. Love is true and honest, kind and sure.

It is often, surprisingly to many, not spontaneous. In my book *Think Love* I explored how we can consciously bring love into all aspects of our lives. It starts with a thought and grows with the energy of positivity. Like a seed pushing its way up through the ground and defying gravity, love is astonishingly strong.

It's this vibrancy that enables not only happiness but moments of joy. Made of positivity, love generates positivity too – it can't help itself – it's what it is.

A friend who has been through two separations exclaimed when he knew I was writing about positivity and love: 'Love isn't positive! It's painful.' I paused before starting to reply and in those few moments, he realized something. 'No,' he said, 'I'm not talking about love am I? I'm talking about being in love, or lust, and the pain of breaking up when it goes wrong. Perhaps I've never truly loved.'

We talked for a long time about the meaning of love. I pointed out that love can indirectly cause pain – for we do inevitably suffer losses, bereavements and disappointments. There are no guarantees that love, any more than the 'in-love' feeling, will be permanently reciprocated by those we love. Nor does it guarantee harmony in relationships and life generally.

But the goodness and energy of love, not just love for our loved ones, but love for the world and all the other kinds of love, is healing, strengthening and inspiring. It will, if we allow it, carry us through grief and misfortune. It enables forgiveness and courage.

Love's vitality is a power-house of energy – but it's up to you to allow it to shine. Just by thinking of love, you let yourself feel love and it's a progressive alchemical reaction – everything you say and do, everyone you come in contact with, will be affected beneficially. You'll work more enthusiastically and so will be more efficient. You'll enjoy your leisure time more.

A friend, Ennis, who is a farmer, told me of a comment another farmer made to him that really made him think. Will is rather dour. He finds life hard and often tedious. He asked Ennis, who always appears cheerful, 'Don't you get tired of having to go out in all weathers to look after the animals and do all the work? Don't you get fed up with it, if you're honest, and wish you didn't have to do it?'

'He took me by surprise,' Ennis told me. 'I wanted to answer honestly so I really thought about it. But my answer, completely truthfully, is that no, I don't ever get tired of it. I love the stock, I enjoy looking after them, and I really do love the work. Obviously in the worst of the weather it's hard. But I don't want to give up, and I always find it satisfying. It's my life and I love it.'

That last phrase works backwards too: it's his love and he lives it. Think love and live love and it lights up the work that we do and the life we live. It starts and continues with a positive attitude. And love, in hand with positivity, adds its on-going vibrancy to all we do.

Get in touch with your spirit and higher power

One of the main reasons so many millions subscribe to a faith is that it gives them the feeling that they are loved, partly by the God or ethos they believe in and also by the like-minded community they're part of. It also gives a conduit for their love to flow out of them and dance in the joy of connecting with their spiritual and sacred side.

Nowadays believing in a higher power, another dimension or, as a friend likes to call it, the greater goodness, is as popular as following an organized religion. Some simply sense the love all around them. There are many conduits and we'll look at this further in Chapter 6.

But it needs to be mentioned here, too, because it's a very special kind of love and when you take the time to be aware of the feeling, and appreciate it to the full – how could you not when it's so good? – it fills your life with a positive current that supports, soothes and inspires you.

When you make a regular practice of connecting with your spirituality, be it through prayer, meditation or simply a listening silence, the feeling that love is all around you as you do so is intense. Try it now:

- ✓ Sit in a comfortable position.
- ✓ Fold your hands in your lap.
- ✓ Be aware of every part of your body from your toes to the tips of your fingers and the top of your head.
- ✓ Breathe slowly and deeply.
- ✓ Give thanks for your life.
- ✓ Find something to praise about your life today.
- ✓ Be aware of the main emotion you're feeling today.
- ✓ If it's sorrow, don't feel you have to hold back tears – let them flow.
- ✓ Feel cradled or just held by the love all around you.
- ✓ Relax into it.
- ✓ Respond with your own loving thankfulness.
- ✓ Stay with the feeling of peace and love for as long as you like.
- ✓ Gently come back 'into the room'.
- ✓ Stretch.
- ✓ Be aware of whether you feel peaceful or energized – perhaps both.

If being in touch with your spirituality is new to you, this practice may take 20 minutes or so. As you get used to it, you'll find you can make the connection much more quickly – even almost instantly.

It may be comforting, it may be inspiring. Breathing and pulse rate slow, muscles relax, tension leaves your face.

I've often introduced this process when counselling and it has a profound healing effect. It also feels a deeply loving way to sense what's right for us and whether we're on the right path.

I can't explain it. I don't know how it works. Perhaps it is a way of accessing information stored in our brain. Perhaps it is a connection with a loving higher power or dimension. But the love you feel as you sit and listen, the love that stays with you afterwards, and the loving understanding or awareness you receive, are comforting and often inspiring. Worth doing, without a doubt.

I talked recently with a woman called Lucy who has followed this spiritual practice for many years. She told me: 'Richard Dawkins and co say there is no God. Perhaps they are right, perhaps not – it seems to me the jury is still out. But, for me, when I do this I feel very strongly that I'm making a connection. I think of it as the energy of love. The cynics say faith is a crutch. Certainly it is for me – very much so! There've been times in my life when I might have gone under if it weren't for the feeling of love that seemed not just to surround me but to carry me through the worst times. When all is well it's like being with an old, extremely good friend who wants, always, the very best for me. It also reminds me to try to live more lovingly and lovably. It's 100 per cent positive and has made an incredible difference to my life. If only they'd teach it in schools, civilization would be transformed into a loving, war-free, humane global culture. Love truly could transform everything.'

Love certainly shines through the dark days as well as the good times. With positivity and love in mind we have emotional poise and fitness. When you are caught in a storm – even the eye of a storm – stay connected, think and be aware. Keeping a sense of perspective, do what's best, changing your behaviour if appropriate but always keeping your personal inner core of love and positivity. They are your strength and protection in difficult times.

Love makes life not just worth living but a journey dappled with gold and thankfulness. Relish its light. Remember to love – giving, transmitting and accepting it. Love has all the answers you need. Take ego out of the equation and it's what you are left with. If everyone understood and practised this, the power of love would right the whole world. But don't underestimate your place, your role, your presence in the world. You are meant to be. Don't fret – simply love; love your world and beyond; love all the living creatures. And always remember, you are much loved too.

Love is the greatest treasure and is at the heart of our well-being. We have this incredible gift of being able to be loving and lovable and it's up to us to recognize and thankfully use it, all the time, transfusing our lives. Love is positivity. It feels good and it is good.

Appreciate the love all around you

The water is ice-cold against the back of my mouth and throat. I give thanks for the gift of fresh, clean water. The dog's ear is soft as velvet on my thigh. She opens her eyes to look at me and goes back to sleep. I stroke her, trying to make my touch as light as thistledown. Such tenderness, such love. I call my aunt to see how she is and hear in her voice the pleasure it gives her. A friend emails me with a nice message.

Such tenderness, such love. Our days are full of small incidents of love and it's so good to appreciate them. Look out for the little bits of love you experience through the day and the way they lift your spirits – they'll soar even higher when you pay attention to them and are thankful.

If love is there in these small things, the universe must be positively crackling with it.

Crackling? Humming. Roaring. Rejoicing. Purring.

Feel it – this presence, this silent hum of pure energy and love. You are part of it. Feel it and you will be at peace and at the same time full of vitality.

How fortunate we are to be here on this earth, now. When so many blessings cascade on us, flow with us, dazzle and beguile.

And all we need to do is smile and be glad.

5

An affinity with the world
and our environment

In this chapter, you'll embrace positivity when you:
- *Appreciate the sense and power of being blessed*
- *Listen to your intuition and inner wisdom*
- *Invite well-being into your life*
- *Relish happiness, joy and bliss on an everyday basis*
- *Encourage a feeling of oneness with creation, humanity and the environment*
- *Gain energy, understanding, peace and strength from meditation and prayer*
- *Absorb energy from the natural world*
- *Live in harmony with the earth and humankind.*

You know that feeling when you feel at one with the world? Maybe you feel as though you're dancing in step with the universe, or suddenly, inexplicably vibrating with a joy that seems to be all around as well as within you? At other times we can feel transfused with a less exciting but nonetheless pleasant feeling of deep peace and belonging. In a wider sense than being happy with our immediate circumstances, it's a feeling of being at home within our planet and the surrounding universe.

Appreciating this sense of connection and belonging gives a feeling of completeness and being at one with life and allows your personal power to light up your life. It also sustains you through life's difficulties and sorrows.

All our powers and senses work individually and together to energize, help, protect and generally enable us to live as well and joyfully as possible. Our sixth sense encompassing, intuition, instinct and general subliminal awareness of what's going on in and around us also enriches and lights up our whole being.

While the feeling of affinity and joy may be serendipitous, it's also yours to invite and welcome into your life every day.

Appreciate the sense of being blessed

We live in an astonishingly complex world with myriad aspects. Nature and human nature are in many ways loving and kind but can also be dangerous and even violent. As our take on all of this is subjective it would be easy to assume that we'd be equally divided on which predominates. Yet a survey has shown that a third of us believe we have a personal guardian angel. Considering we live in an increasingly secular society, that's a remarkably high statistic. For many, then, this translates as a feeling that we are somehow individually protected and lovingly cared for – angels being a metaphor for a loving presence in the world that we feel is there but can't explain.

How many more of us feel blessed in all kinds of ways, much of the time, without that very particular focused belief? I expect at least another third of us. That's just wonderful, isn't it? So much gladness, hope, encouragement and an over all feeling of being loved – all there in our human consciousness.

But here's the most exciting thing of all: how many more of us have the ability to feel protected and beloved by, if you like, the universe, and can activate or increase the feeling at will? I believe all of us, for it's one of the powers of positive thinking.

It isn't about make-believe. We have the natural instinct and we have the ability to use it in our lives, every day. Positivity simply links the two, opening us up to the comfort, peace and sometimes sheer joy of feeling we are lovingly watched over and looked after.

Sensing this gives us confidence in others and in ourselves. It's all too easy to listen to or read the news and take in the false impression that most people are corrupt. By keeping in touch with our faith in our own and others' essential good nature, we keep a healthy perspective, as ill deeds only make the news because they are not the norm.

A criminal lawyer, Helen, told me: 'After I'd been doing this work for a few months I became depressed. The cases I was dealing with – or rather the criminals involved in them – were vile and they began to colour my view of humanity in a palette from grey to black. Thankfully a wise senior partner put it in perspective for me. He said we have to remember that for every thousand criminals there are hundreds of thousands of law-abiding citizens. The vast majority of these are naturally good, honest people. Even the criminals, he believes, are rarely if ever there because they are intrinsically nasty but because they haven't been taught or haven't understood what's right and wrong behaviour, or circumstances have channelled them in the direction of crime.

'Now when I'm working with these people, I remember the wealth of goodness and kindness in the world. I work as a volunteer with ex-convicts to help them not just to take their place in their home community, but to appreciate how good it feels. When they marry this with the feeling of being themselves protected by a guardian angel, they are transformed by a feeling of belonging, both in their home patch and the wider world, often for the first time in their lives.'

The feeling of being blessed by our own caring, responsible attitude and by being lovingly watched over is transformational. We don't have to wait until we're older and contemplating our mortality – we can sense the 'guardian angel' feeling at any time of our lives.

It isn't a case of there being an interventionist god ready to perform miracles to help us avoid problems. I wish! It's that this extraordinary sense of feeling protected is there, constantly, for us, whatever trials and tribulations we face in life. We sense, as Julian of Norwich said: 'And all shall be well, and all manner of thing shall be well.' It gives us an abidingly positive peace and strength and feels sublime.

Listen to your intuition and inner wisdom

Intuition and inner wisdom are another aspect of our inner knowledge. They broaden and deepen our understanding and insight and are a feel-good part of our well-being.

As adults we've learned to rationalize and be logical. We try hard to be scientific and sceptical of anything that is not exact. All this is fine as long as it goes in tandem with the intuition and wisdom or gut feeling we're born with. They are great gifts that too often we forget or deny. What an advantage we miss out on when we do that – what treasure that's yours to mine when you recognize these heaven-sent forms of intelligence and let them enlighten your understanding.

We hear a lot in techno speak these days about controls for computers, machines, gizmos and gadgets being 'intuitive'. When they are, they're so much easier to use. In much the same pleasurable, relaxed way, so is life much easier to live when we follow our inbuilt intuitive resources. It only takes a moment or two to tune in to them:

- ✓ Pause.
- ✓ Check out your overall impression of the situation.
- ✓ Do you have any express physical sensation?
- ✓ Is your body language telling you something?
- ✓ What awareness do you have?
- ✓ Is there a message about what's going on?
- ✓ Is there a realization of the best way to proceed?

Don't worry if this sounds time-consuming or clunky – as you become practised in listening to your intuition you'll cover all these steps in a moment's pause. The way our awareness develops, too, is immensely satisfying as we realize how often it helps us avoid causing or feeling hurt, understand the relationship or group dynamic, or simply relax and enjoy ourselves. Instead of life being a seemingly difficult puzzle, fraught with hazards that we struggle to negotiate successfully, situations are surprisingly clear, making it so much easier to defuse or solve problems and enjoy ourselves without feeling as though we're on an obstacle course.

Much of the time it means we can relax in the knowledge we're not missing warning signs, and be enjoyably happy-go-lucky and confident.

In patently difficult, or edgy, or potentially difficult situations, intuition is again useful, but we can also call on innate and learned wisdom to figure out a comprehensive understanding and be our own advisor and consultant.

As an agony aunt, I first look at the situation as it's described to me, then I try to review it from the viewpoint of everyone else involved.

Then, holistically, I reflect on the most appropriate and useful advice or guidance. So far all very practical, positive and constructive. But there is often a further ingredient of truly helpful advice – overall intuition and wisdom. Having worked out possible practical solutions, I take a moment – as above – to listen to my gut feeling about the situation and the mindsets of those involved. Often it backs up the commonsense approach but sometimes an awareness overrides that and you suddenly realize what the best answer is.

Often, too, intuition and wisdom recognize or highlight an existing spiritual element or need. There is more on this throughout Chapter 6.

Apart from the positive benefits of using intuition and wisdom to help you live as simply and as much without stress as possible, paying attention to them feels good in itself. It means you are listening to and valuing yourself. One client who learned to pause and allow her intuition and wisdom to come into play said:

> 'It blew me away when I realized that I was intuitive. I'd never thought of myself like that, and I'd often been secretly envious of people who could divine things from a situation that I was oblivious to. As I started practising pausing and just being aware, like you described, it was like the picture being coloured in. Sometimes it would happen immediately – sometimes different aspects would be coloured and clarified later in the day. I'd find myself thinking 'Ah…of course…'or 'Oh my goodness, now I understand what's going on.' Over and over again it stopped me from putting my foot in it, which I'd had a tendency to do, or from acting in some way unhelpful to the situation. I feel and behave much more empathically now and get on so much better with people. Best of all, I like myself more – I've become far more thoughtful and caring – the person I'd like to have been – and now am!'

Invite well-being into your life

Steady inner happiness, contentment and a healthy, healing attitude are the main ingredients for well-being and all three, with their various components, are yours to welcome and safeguard in your life. All depend on you to invite them in, every day.

Before exploring this further, I'd like to take a look at the down-turns of life in case you or someone you know is suffering one now.

Can we honestly experience well-being in such times? Yes, to some extent we can as the energy for positivity is always there for us. In the fine weather of naturally happy days it's the wind in your sails as you bat along enjoying the trip. In a dismal, frightening storm you have to fight the storm or batten down the hatches – but even then, positive power is there to help you survive and even enjoy moments of laughter, camaraderie, etc., as you do.

And however bleak circumstances may be, they'll be much easier to cope with if you remain positive. It tops up your energy reserves for one thing, while a negative approach is draining. Even in the worst of times – perhaps especially in them – being as positive as possible is helpful, even if it's just hanging onto the fact that you will get through this and it will be better for everyone around you too if you stay stable. Asking in your mind for help and strength gives you instant strength and comfort, as does feeling the memory of active happiness when it's presently deserted you.

None of this is denying the need to experience any loss, grief and illness to the full, but while you're in that place your mind and body will be naturally working to heal you and the positivity of realizing this and helping the process as best you can is comforting and sustaining for you and may be a lifeline for those around you too.

Keeping a sense of being cared for, as described in the first section of this chapter, is also hugely comforting and soothing, and meditation and prayer are direct routes to this feeling of peace. There is more on this later in this chapter.

Let's look now at our normal days when there are no major problems and we can rejoice about our good fortune.

Rejoice about our good fortune? This isn't something we tend to do unless we've had a stroke of good luck or been successful in some way. And yet we are so fortunate on an everyday basis. We not only have life but we have consciousness of it. We have the means to enjoy it. We have all the elements of the ability to be positive, including the sixth sense that connects us with the energy behind our universe, another dimension that gives us strength, comfort and joy and which we can tune in to at any time.

Sometimes it helps us appreciate our blessings if we compare them to those of people who lack them. As ever, there are two ways of looking at this – negative and positive – but even an initially negative attitude can be turned into a constructive, good outcome with some thought. This was brought home to me recently by the difference between two people I'd been discussing well-being with – one a friend, the other a person I was counselling. Both were tired of life and, while not seriously depressed, fed up with what they saw as a day-to-day struggle despite being prosperous and having no current difficulties. This is an increasing problem in the West's materialistic culture where over-abundance, if not appreciated and shared, can make us depressed.

I suggested that a good way to get our everyday existence into perspective and appreciate our well-being is to think of those far less fortunate, for instance those with few of the resources we take for granted, let alone luxuries, as well as those who are going through extreme difficulties. They agreed to do this and contrast it with the essential good fortune they themselves had.

Next time I saw Cerys, she looked doleful and said she was still feeling low. I asked her if she'd tried my suggestion: 'Yes,' she answered, 'But thinking about all those unfortunate people just made me feel even more depressed.'

It had had the opposite effect on Paul, who said: 'It made me feel a lot more positive as I realized what a lot I have to be grateful for. I've determined not to let myself get so negative in future and I'm going to do more to help aid and relief charities.'

Two attitudes – one looking, much out of habit, on the negative side, the other deliberately choosing and being uplifted by the positive.

But Cerys saw the irony in her reaction, and decided she wanted to learn to look for the potential in situations. While comparing her life to others less fortunate than her didn't work for her, it did make her realize she had a deep longing to do something active and constructive to help them. She began working as a volunteer and fundraiser and loves it. She's also thinking of looking for work abroad with a welfare organization.

There are many ways to think positively and we all need to find those that are right for us. Well-being is ours to sense, ours to appreciate, ours to give thanks for – above all, ours to share.

Relish happiness, joy and bliss everyday

One of my favourite people used to be a moaner. He looked on the black side of everything, finding something to grumble about in even the sunniest of situations and his prophecies of doom were legendary. Happy he was not. But then he had a change of attitude. I don't know for sure, but I suspect that when a couple of his elderly friends died it jolted him into appreciating how precious and good his longevity is. Suddenly he stopped moaning about anything and everything and instead talked of happy memories, nice things happening in the present, and hopes of future plans. His face changed from Mr Grump to a cheerful enough if not exactly ecstatic demeanour (well – that would have been miraculous!)

Why am I telling you this story? Because so often people go on about how leopards can't change their spots, along these lines: 'I should be on that television show *Grumpy Old Women/Men*. I can't help my personality, it's how I am. It's just me – I can't change. Happy? No one can *make* themselves happy.'

Wrong, wrong and wrong. We can change our personality – it isn't about inventing something. It's about reverting to the essential love of life we were born with. And happiness is a state of being that is dependent on attitude. We choose to look for the bright side of any situation. We choose to think happy thoughts. We choose, whatever our age, to resist the temptation to be a grumpy so-and-so. We choose to spread love, light and joy. And, in doing so, we suddenly, miraculously, amazingly find that actually we are happy. All in the mind? The choosing yes, absolutely, but the result is 100 per cent real.

Joy is a bit different. It's happiness certainly but of a blissful, elevated kind. It's about sheer delight. A little bit – or a lot – of heaven.

It's commonly experienced when we're 'in love' or inebriated with some other drug but we can introduce it into our lives with positive thinking and by finding out our own triggers for this magical state. Music and other art forms, love of all kinds, nature, physical or work achievement, beauty, spirituality – some passive, some active – all these and many others can lift us up spontaneously and render us joyful.

Noticing the feeling and giving it our full attention is key to appreciating it to the full. And when we do that – really focus, really exult – we release more feel-good hormones and pave the way for experiencing the state more and more often.

This is such a fascinating and enticing point. Emotional 'muscles' are like physical ones – the more we exercise them, the stronger and more supple they become. The more we practise thinking positively, the more positive we become. Same with happiness, same with joy.

We don't need to 'manufacture' happiness – we have it at our disposal. It's an inborn gift that's often unnoticed, ignored or even denied. But it's there to choose – and the more we do that the easier it is to be happy as a matter of course.

Brian, a journalist, told me why he'd for many years chosen the alternative – a downbeat, negative, gloomy attitude to life: 'When I started in the news room, the atmosphere (except when a scoop was breaking) was of discontent. I was in great awe of these people, seeing them as old-timers and experts. I thought they were so cool, and though disappointed that they weren't enthusiastic about their jobs and life generally, I followed their lead and adopted their mind-set of cynicism and dissatisfaction.

'But recently I realized that this habitual mind-set had finally led me into chronic depression. An old friend told me straight that I'd changed from the cheerful, inspired young man he'd known and become a real grouch. He said I'd better change back and no one could do it for me. That's why I'm here. I don't want to be like this any more. I want to enjoy life again before it's too late.'

We talked about the nature of positivity and he agreed to give some of the principles looked at in this book a go. Soon he found he was looking at his colleagues, and anyone else who'd assumed a grey persona, in a different light.

'It isn't clever or cool,' he said. 'And it wasn't the real me, most definitely. I can't even claim that they'd brainwashed me – I'd brainwashed myself. Learning to be true to my real nature wasn't nearly as hard as I thought it would be – in fact it's been a breeze. It feels completely different to have a positive approach and to admit to happiness in good fortune and hope and optimism when things go wrong. It feels good. So simple and I can't tell you how glad I am that my old buddy drew me up short and you helped me find the way.'

We can't, it's true, be happy all the time. As sensitive, emotional creatures we're all affected by life's vicissitudes and it's natural and right that we should respond to them honestly. But from the lows, even the deepest ones, we can reach up and pull ourselves out, especially when we accept the help of others and the energy of positivity and love.

And strange though it may sound, we often appreciate even the downs of life in retrospect, for the wisdom and emotional depth gained in them. They also provide a valuable contrast, enabling us to appreciate and enjoy happier times completely and unreservedly.

Sometimes life is a roller-coaster and you just have to hang on for dear life. Sometimes it's a bit like skiing down a run you're comfortable with and can thoroughly enjoy. Sometimes you're pretty much stationary and content with the peace and calm. Always, a positive take on life, wherever and however you are, feels good and gives you precious energy.

Here are some daily steps for feel-good positivity:

✓ Look for the goodness around you and allow it to impress itself on you.
✓ Be aware of any evil and ugliness but don't let it invade you.
✓ Praise others for their talent and goodness at any opportunity.
✓ Sense your personal power shining bright.
✓ Smile often.
✓ Laugh. If there's nothing to laugh about – find something!
✓ Reach out a hand to someone who may need it – or may not but no matter.
✓ Look kindly on yourself and give yourself an imaginary hug.

Positivity lets us experience heaven on earth, every day.

Encourage a feeling of oneness with creation

Existential awareness is the boon or bane of our lives, depending how we view it. Looked at negatively, it can fill us with anxiety. Individuality is challenging, certainly, and knowing that one day we will no longer be alive at least in the way we are now, inhabiting a body and brain, fills many with such dread that the subject of death has become almost taboo.

But oh how liberating it is when we see it positively as part of our natural lifecycle and nothing to be frightened of. With this attitude of positivity to all stages of our life, there is a refreshing sense that we are fitting in exactly as we are supposed to, part of the wonderful patchwork planet we live in and love. And it gives us a great incentive to appreciate every day of our life and make the most of it.

There is much warm encouragement to explore and nurture our individuality. At the same time each one of us is part of this extraordinarily complex world and humanity in an age when civilization is growing in knowledge exponentially. The potential for us to be at one with our environment and our fellow creatures locally and globally is greater than ever before. So much possibility. Feel the excitement of it. Feel the wonder and be full of awe at our good fortune to live in this exhilarating time of discovery.

There is no room, of course, for complacency. The current cultures and civilizations of the world are by no means all well intentioned, but enough people are seeking to work together for the good of all and to explore the possibilities for protecting our environment to give us tremendous hope for the future. Ultimately we are simply going to have to work together on a global basis to ensure the survival of our species and other life forms and our planet too. Already, as global realization of this develops, rogue governments are falling and nations are increasingly working together. There is a growing sense that we need to develop and share our knowledge, wisdom and resources.

And there is a lot each of us can do, both in joining others in solidarity to work together, promoting good practices, and also individually, making a difference in myriad ways.

It's an on-going learning curve for most of us. Each day we may find ourselves thinking 'But I'm so small and un-influential, I can't make a difference,' or alternatively feeling that we do and then berating ourselves for being arrogant and stupid to have that feeling when we are so inconsequential! But it's in such conversations, internally and with friends, that we learn and grow and bolster our positivity and confidence in today's and the future's possibilities. As a friend who lives halfway across the world emailed me:

> *How can we as little individuals stand up against prejudice?*
> *We can make our own existences as good as we can. But maybe*

it is the few that live an innocent hopefulness that keep it all together...and essentially I feel that there are more of us out there than we ever dreamed of...they just need a reminder – and to be reminded that their thoughts are not special or alone...and encouragement is so vital.

Jacelyn Sims

On a local, everyday practical note, we can get a feeling of oneness and at the same time enjoy the magical feeling of wonder by simply walking in the areas we live in and feeling the atmosphere.

In cities, towns, suburbs and villages:

- ✓ Sense the community and love around you.
- ✓ Look at the buildings and think of the people who planned, designed and built them.
- ✓ Think of the infrastructure and the centuries of thought and work that have brought them to today's level, when they serve so many more thousands of people than the original designers would have ever dreamed.
- ✓ Reflect on your position, today – now – as a part of this intricate picture.
- ✓ Appreciate how you fit in to it – a perfectly crafted piece of the stunning jigsaw.

In the countryside:

- ✓ Sense the power and love of nature.
- ✓ Look at the scenery, the trees and vegetation, the views.
- ✓ Consider what is natural, what has been grown or planned by man.
- ✓ Think of the context of what you are seeing and experiencing today, considering the history of this place and the people and animals who have walked here through the ages.
- ✓ Reflect on your good fortune in being here, enjoying and marvelling at the multi-faceted beauty.
- ✓ Appreciate how you fit in to it – you are here, taking your place in the tapestry of life at this particular moment.

Feel, at the same time, pride and humility. It's fine to be proud that you, as an individual – a unique being – are taking your place in this amazing world. It's fine, too, to be overcome with the wonder that you, such an infinitely small, in physical terms at least, piece in the great scheme of things are taking it all in and adding to the positivity of the planet.

Benefit from meditation and prayer

When we meditate, we exist purely in the moment. If nothing else, it gives you a time of peace. As we get used to it, the calm deepens – it's more relaxing than sleep, and you can use the space of quiet, free of worries and stress, to experience a sensation of healing, or to listen for guidance from your inner wisdom or beyond.

It also triggers creativity. Ideas tend to flow after meditation.

Meditating is completely positive. It doesn't matter whether or not you have a religious faith. It isn't 'new age' or any kind of cult. It's simply a time honoured practice of entering into the quiet and letting go of busy, demanding thoughts.

I recommend it unreservedly. It's a tonic – like drinking a glass of positivity and healing elixir.

For many years in my last home neighbours used to come round once a week and we'd meditate for half an hour or so, then ask for healing for ourselves and our loved ones. Then we'd put the world to rights over a glass or cup of something nice by the fire in winter, or watching the sun set on summer evenings. Our little meditation group was a powerful, enriching oasis of peace, friendship, compassion, understanding and last but not least laughter and we all miss it. But life moves on and we were scattered and now live too far from one another to get together. Perhaps one day we'll live near enough to each other again. I hope so.

Currently I meditate with family and friends when possible, enjoying the sense of like-minded togetherness and solidarity. But I also love to meditate alone which is good in its own way. On my own I simply sit silently and slip into meditation. That's how it feels – like easing imperceptibly between the dimensions to a glade of light and love between the worlds. As a group, we'd start the meditation by listening to a guided visualization and then sit for the remainder of the time with some non-demanding music in the background. Some like to chant, some to repeat a mantra – any word of your choice – in their mind. Whatever works for you is fine. In Chapter 6 there are descriptions of the different sorts of meditation and you may find you have a particular liking and rapport with one particular one, or like to use different techniques at different times.

Prayer is very similar to meditation and often the two converge and overlap, fusing in love and peace. To differentiate, one way is to think of meditation as listening, prayer as requesting help.

Again, anyone can pray, you don't need to have a faith and even if you're an atheist prayer is a positive practice with many benefits. To whom are you praying if so? Non-believers in anything other than our science-proven reality can simply suspend dis-belief or choose to think of it in terms of praying to their subconscious and wisdom. Asking for guidance and help is therapeutic in its own right. There is a peace-giving energy to it, just as there is when you meditate. In the darkest hour the cry for help is always heard. The answer or other help may not come instantly and often comes in an unexpected way you couldn't have imagined, but come it will. I think again of the story of the man who contemplated his solitary footsteps in the sand as he walked through a troubled time and berated God for not being there when needed only to realize that the footprints were God's who was carrying him. We'll look more at prayer and meditation in Chapter 6.

Whether or not we have a faith, meditation and prayer both give the sense of being carried or held safely. It's a wonderful feeling. Life affirming, love affirming. Healing, strengthening.

Apart from this, they feel good. Positivity, unlimited. Enjoy!

Absorb positivity from the natural world

How calm and accepting nature is. The cycle of life turns through birth, death and birth again – on and on – and it is only we humans who get in a strop about it. Everything else lives uncomplainingly and un-worryingly and contemplating this and to some extent adopting their natural attitude can help us to be calmer and more accepting too.

Getting outside, every day if possible, enables us to soak up the energy of life that pulses all around us. We may josh about tree-huggers, but walk among trees, touch them, lean against them, sit quietly underneath and gaze up at the canopy of leaves and branches and you will sense their majesty and power as their tremendous life force sends the sap through them. It's wonderful to walk in woods and forests in the countryside but you don't have to leave town to feel and appreciate the beauty and strength of trees for every town and suburb has a park, golf course or square where trees – young or ancient, it doesn't matter – grow.

The feeling of positivity they emanate will come across to you strongly if you take time to look at them, really look and register their beauty and timelessness.

Gardens are an amazing source of positive energy too. Whether you're an active gardener or simply enjoy the pleasures of being in a garden, you can revel in the sense of growth, the beauty all around you, the colours that make your heart sing. Notice it all. Notice every tiny details of the extraordinary complexity of nature, and at the same time the bigger picture – how all the plants seem to work together in harmony, resonating with your appreciation and love. I once read that if you visit a herb garden at dawn you can see the aura of the herbs dancing above them. I've done so several times and my spirit dances with it – Imagination? Fancy? I've no idea – perhaps it is – but whether or not that's true it's a wonderful vision and feeling that puts you in a brilliantly good mood at the start of the day!

Gardens have known therapeutic properties too. I remember, many years ago, talking with a woman, Sue, I'd been introduced to at a social gathering. Unknown to her, I'd been through a traumatic time and was very fragile. Because you don't normally go around telling new acquaintances your troubles, I was talking with her brightly about this and that. So it surprised me as we were saying goodbye when she looked very directly at me, handed me a slip of paper with an address on it and said: 'Come and visit us – we have access to the gardens next door. You don't have to talk to anyone unless you want to.' I was speechless – she clearly had intuited my inner emotional pain and was holding out a hand of help. 'Come tomorrow,' she said. 'You'll be welcome.'

Telling myself I need only pop in for a coffee, I went round the next morning. After greeting me warmly but quietly she showed me the way through to the neighbouring gardens which were at the time well known for their charm and often open to the public. Whether or not there were others there I don't remember, but the feeling of peace, love and beauty flood over me again as I write. I stayed there for the rest of the day, wandering around absorbing the atmosphere, or simply sitting or standing still. I realized how incredibly tired I was, worn out with the sorrow and shock of the last few weeks. And a seemingly magical thing happened. It was as though I was being washed through with a tender, healing balm. The garden seemed to hold me lovingly and I felt safe and cherished. At the same time the emotional weight I'd been carrying was lifted.

Since then I've realized that it wasn't 'magical'. Help and healing is available to all of us, all the time. People will help us if we let them. And we can always find an oasis of peace where nature will heal us.

Perhaps there is another natural phenomenon at work here too. Throughout my life I've often been struck by the feeling of healing power and energy of certain places. Throughout history this has been annotated by writers – Wordsworth in particular felt the sense of connection and inspiration such places give us. It can be a scene of beauty, a viewpoint across countryside, a garden, a churchyard. Some say such places have physical therapeutic properties as there is a particularly strong magnetic current there. Others claim that they are points where ley lines cross each other.

I don't think it matters why or how it works – it's enough that it does. It's intensely positive, wondrously therapeutic, truly intrinsically healing. There are many physical health benefits from being outside and more on this in Chapter 7.

Boating on or walking by moving water, be it a river or the sea, is an exceptionally positive experience where the sound is as therapeutic as the beauty and perhaps the moisture or ozone in the air has a calming effect as well. Animals who are ill or very elderly are often to be found by a river or stream if one flows through their pasture. Vets say the moisture in the air makes their breathing easier. Perhaps, too, they find peace in the sound and the feeling of timelessness just as we do. They may also sense there is a positive energy, just as there is in gardens and other beautiful natural places.

Whenever you find yourself in a place that's beautiful or feels somehow special:

- ✓ Be aware of any particularly peaceful, inspiring, beautiful or healing atmosphere you're sensing.
- ✓ Pay attention to it.

- ✓ Feel the way it's resonating with you.
- ✓ Appreciate it and love it.
- ✓ Allow yourself to soak up the energy.
- ✓ Feel how your own positive energy and healing power is being boosted.

Appreciate a sense of place and unity

This is our planet. We don't own it. We don't have dominion over other human beings or any creatures. It is the home in which we find ourselves and we are incredibly fortunate to be here.

Home – our resting place, sanctuary, haven. Our base, our oasis.

The earth is all of these, for all of us. You know that wonderful feeling when your home is looking nice and you're pleased to be there? Just as we value and care for our individual dwelling places, so we feel content and uplifted when we value and look after our whole environment locally, nationally, globally and, as time goes by, the reachable universe too.

We are amazingly fortunate to be here at this point in Earth's timeline when resources are still generously available, humanity is generally civilized (or at least trying hard to be!) and we are experiencing the rewards of a communications system and other technology that were until a few years ago unimaginable.

When we disrespect the earth, or perhaps don't consider it at all, we show a lack of respect for ourselves and we do the environment – and ourselves – a disservice. For its goodness and riches to survive, it's vital that we respect it and cherish it – not just a handful of thinking leaders but each and every one of us. And when you do you reap such rewards. You have a sense of being united on a higher level and there's a great feeling of hope, purpose and solidarity. Loving this place, this world and all the life it supports goes full circle around and through it in a life line – a love line – of positive energy.

It's natural – a birth gift – to love the place that welcomed us to this life. It's natural to love the world and all its beauty, ugliness, joy, sorrow – all its complexity and simplicity, the astonishing energy of it all. Such a life force. Such a wonder.

How can it be that we are part of life on this planet? It's so vast in our everyday consciousness, but so tiny a part of the known universe let alone its full scope, of which we can only dream.

It is, literally, everything to us. Whether or not you believe in an after-life or contemplate the possibility of parallel universes, pause for a moment now and every now and then in future, to appreciate our completely – as far as we know – serendipitous place in this extraordinary world:

- ✓ Be still in body and mind.
- ✓ Feel the air all around you and in every breath you take.
- ✓ Sense your whole body from the tips of your toes to the top of your head.
- ✓ Picture the globe and see the area where you are.
- ✓ Realize that you are there – now – this moment.
- ✓ Contemplate with awe how tiny a speck you are in relation to the whole world.
- ✓ Joy in the knowledge that no matter how relatively physically small, you are a living being full of energy and positivity in your own right.
- ✓ Think how valuable a person you can be in your own patch, your own community.
- ✓ And how, in being your best self, you inevitably make a positive impact, an impression and a difference to the world and its goodness.

Live in harmony with the earth and humankind

Having a rapport with our world and all its wildlife and plants – or at least having respect for those we can't warm to – feels intrinsically right and good.

If we behave selfishly in a way that doesn't harmonize with the environment and perhaps actually harms it, we don't feel good inside. Sure, there may be passing thrills and pleasures, but overall we feel grubby. Follow a path where instead you care about and benefit the world and all its life and you'll feel completely different – more confident, responsible, loving and lovable – in all you'll feel you're a valuable presence here and that feels extremely positive and energizing. It's cool and it's buzzy!

There are myriad ways to live well on a practical level – ways that will benefit the environment wherever we live – in cities or the countryside. Here are a few that will make you feel lighter – and enlightened:

- ✓ Live a little or a lot more simply, looking to shop for things that are useful rather than status symbols.
- ✓ Give up obsessions or addictions or anything that's threatening to become one. That includes compulsive use of mobile phones, computer games, etc.!
- ✓ Be generous. Whenever you find yourself feeling possessive, envious, jealous or greedy, give something away.
- ✓ Enjoy the beautiful landscapes and all the life of the world without feeling you have to dominate or own it.
- ✓ As far as possible, live within your means.
- ✓ If you eat meat, know that it is a great luxury and have respect for the animal it's from.
- ✓ Reduce your unnecessary use of the earth's limited resources like water and fuel for transport and heating.
- ✓ Treat all life with respect.
- ✓ Volunteer or do something else positive to help in some way.

This is our home. The most extraordinarily stunning world imaginable. It offers everything for our survival. It is up to us – each one of us – to work individually and together to look after it for ourselves in the present and for the generations who will follow us. When we do our hearts sing and the energy our positivity generates is mind-blowingly powerful.

Now and every day – pause to feel awe and great gladness that you are here on this earth and that you are part of it. Feel the wonder of this and be full of praise and thankfulness.

6

Noticing and nurturing your spirituality

In this chapter, you'll embrace positivity when you:
- *Develop a relationship with your spiritual side*
- *Take an interest in the concept of the divine*
- *Follow the spiritual path that's right for you*
- *Appreciate the positive power of prayer*
- *Meditate the way that's right for you*
- *Practise the magic of praise and spiritual wonder*
- *Joy in the sense of the sacred*
- *Understand the presence of heaven on earth*
- *Show up, be present and live in the moment.*

Spirituality is important to us whether or not we are religious as it's a link that releases us from the boundaries of the universe and its physics. Free of these inhibitions, our natural instinct, which deeply understands that we each have a soul, can notice and nurture it and bring the positive energy of the spiritual sense into our lives more and more. We can also reach beyond our understanding of and relationship with this world to the sense we have of something other that's good and loving.

Our spirituality helps us understand ourselves and feel at one with our being, leading us to inner contentment, happiness and joy. It often overlaps with the affinity with the world we experience through our other senses, as explored in the last chapter, but it isn't the same. It's a sense – and in a way a language – that we were born with. It is much about love, too and in fact it comes into all aspects of our positivity, if we let it. We are, at our very core, spiritual beings and, although we can function without paying attention to it, it is a powerfully positive and astonishingly helpful through life's journey if we want it to be.

Develop a relationship with your spiritual side

Spirituality is the feeling and expression of the spirit of life we all have and the soul that gives us consciousness of it. Books have been written on the difference between spirit and soul but I will leave this discourse to the theologians. Essentially I feel they are the same thing and in this book I use them interchangeably.

You may like to try right now how it feels to accept their presence. Seek this blessing and it will be with you.

Find a few moments to take a break from the hustle and bustle of life and while you pause:

- ✓ Seek to sense that your soul is your essence and your spirit.
- ✓ Feel this elemental life force.
- ✓ Sense what a wonderful part of you it is.
- ✓ Be aware of a positive charge of inspiration, energy, or a deep feeling of peace or all three together, following on from each other.

The more we practise touching base with our spirituality like this or in any way, the easier it becomes. The feeling of warmth, support and deep love is there for us whatever our faith and in the absence of one too, whenever we wish to let it light up our lives or support us through troubles. It's very positive and can fill us with energy that carries us through the rest of the day even though we may previously have felt tired or lacklustre.

But however natural this feels and however uplifting and healing, we're sure to sometimes question it ourselves or have doubts put into our minds by others.

Is there really such a thing as a life force within us that isn't dependent on the physical body – that rises above it and connects with another dimension and perhaps, many think, the source of our being?

Science hasn't quite fathomed it yet and even some of our top thinkers move between belief or strong suspicion that there is such a life force and conviction that there isn't. The truth, as I write this, is that they have no idea what reality is, and neither quantum science nor the notion of the 'Big Bang' explain it. As Brian Cox in *The Wonders of the Universe* points out, the theory of the Big Bang only takes us back to that point in time. There are so many fascinating questions: What was before? And, as I'm always thinking: What other dimensions may there be? What other universes? Can the sense many of us have that there is something more be simply caused by chemicals in the brain? Scientists have no more idea of the answers than any of us. One scientist's recent idea is that our world and reality is a hologram projected from the edge of the universe – but surely most of us have had this idea, it's hardly new. Other scientists continue to think the concept of parallel universes may be the answer.

Scientific knowledge is growing exponentially but it's possible that the human brain and even the latest quantum computers will simply not develop during our lifetime, if ever, the kind of intelligence or scope to fully understand the mystery of life as we experience it.

But research has shown that a part of the human brain is geared up to seek communication with our source and an understanding of our spirit, and to try to connect, usually through prayer and worship. It's inherent in our psyche and our subconscious has a deep knowledge of a spiritual link to the other currently un-understandable dimension, the mystery of what else there is besides our universe. The more we become aware of this sense and pay attention to it the more it infuses us with its positivity, supporting us and lighting up our lives. It's a profound, enriching part of our being and our positivity. It sings a song of deep sorrow and at the same time sublime joy.

It seems to me that when we are aware of this sense we are linking with something – a much, much, much higher intelligence that is above all good and loving and sacred. Many call this God – but as I don't think it necessarily has anything to do with any particular religion and certainly not man-made religious doctrine, I'm cautious about calling it God or religion.

I am referring to awareness of our spirit and soul and the connection we sense to a numinous, benevolent intelligence or dimension beyond the present understanding of our universe. I've mentioned before some of the titles others have for it – the greater goodness, the higher power, the greater consciousness, the mystery, destiny, the wonder, the loving source, the greater wisdom or the sacred sense. Historically it's been called God, the Tao or Dao, Nirvana or Brahman. I don't want to put anyone off reading this chapter, so please bear with me when I talk about God or 'the sacred sense' or one of the other descriptions – and if you prefer substitute in your mind the title that means most to you.

Taking the simplest approach to our spirituality, we can be content to bask, without thinking much about it, in the knowledge of being loved and cared by something that transcends the universe and connects us with the sacred sense.

Whether or not we consider ourselves spiritual, most of us experience at some stage of life, and many persistently throughout, a longing to find our reason for being and our true beginning and to connect with it spiritually. No doubt this wild need is in our genes and it may well have been further developed over the millennia through the practice of religions foisted on us by the various cultures and authorities over the ages, but it's indisputable that we do have the essential instinct that there is something else beyond our world. It's baffling, a mystery and we are fascinated with it. Atheists, agnostics and religious believers alike love to discuss and debate it. All of us, if we take the brakes off our scepticism and our fear of seeming scientifically naïve, can sense the love and life-power of our spirit's beginning and home. All of us can benefit richly and joyously from the connection.

Many travel the world going from guru to guru, seeking to develop their spirituality and find the sacred sense. They learn a lot along the way and the spiritual journey can be hugely rewarding. But you don't actually need to search for your spirituality or the sacred sense. Nor do you need to join any kind of religious club or institution. All it takes is to be aware of it – in a sense tuning in to and walking hand in hand with the love we feel when we open ourselves to it.

You don't need to go to India or the Far East. While fully engaging with normal life – your life and the life all around you, the world you live in, your home, your community, your loved ones – while being a positive, active participant in all this, you can be at one with the mystery of life, the universe and the sacred sense.

You can be spiritually aware at any time, but the most usual ways are through meditation and prayer, in quiet contemplation and when we are uplifted or otherwise deeply moved by something that lifts us out of ourselves – art, for instance, or a momentously emotional experience.

When you want to extend the connection we tried above during times like these, you can encourage it this way:

- ✓ Feel that you are reaching up with your whole spirit to your life source. (It doesn't matter whether or not you have a clear sense of this – just feel yourself reaching up.)
- ✓ Feel the deep peace of connection.
- ✓ Be aware of the current of life that runs through you.
- ✓ Sense the reciprocal joy and love all around you.
- ✓ Listen and wait in pure contentment. You are sitting in the presence of spiritual love and positivity and it feels wondrous.

Take an interest in the concept of the divine

Men of power are but a puff of smoke. What is consistent is the soul's search for the divine. Let that be my guiding star.

Anon

Divinity – the word sounds a bit archaic. For many of us it was a weekly lesson at school which would now be called something like religious education. We thought it essentially boring, but nice in that it didn't tax our young minds too much. But think about the definition of the noun for a moment, *the divine:* 'that which is divine; a Godlike being; of supreme intelligence or worth; splendid; perfect'. And the verb *divine:* 'to perceive or understand as though by a supernatural sense or power'. If we'd had that as the starting point, each lesson would have been transformed – just think how fascinated we'd have been, how our minds would have enjoyed being stretched. Riveting stuff and uplifting – astonishingly uplifting…

For when we take a positive interest in the idea of the divine, it's about allowing ourselves to connect spiritually with the presence we sense lies behind our universe. We don't understand it and we can't prove it exists – and perhaps we won't be able to in our lifetime. But we know in the heart of our being and loving that it is more powerful and good than our wildest conception. It's behind all the energy of positivity and love. It knows every tear that falls, every sparrow that dies and grieves, but it sings with us too in our joys and dances with us in our wonder at the beauty and grace all around us.

It's potent, captivating, deliciously beguiling and beyond our comprehension in its complexity. And yet when we allow ourselves, we feel we somehow know it, and we love it and long to connect with it more than anything else.

Spend a bit more time contemplating your relationship with the divine (there's another name!) and you'll enrich your life as you develop a feeling of oneness with it and at the same time learn so much about yourself.

If, on the other hand, you like to fill in the detail and explore every turn in all things in life, you'll probably do this on the spiritual front too, researching different religions, theology and spiritual philosophy. For you it may be a good idea to slow down, taking as vibrant an interest as ever, but pausing to feel the wonder and mystery of it all and taking time to enjoy your connection.

When we think of and, in our minds, converse with the divine, we naturally orientate ourselves towards goodness and love – the great positive powers of our world. Try it now or any time when you feel like reaching out and communicating with an incredibly generous and infinite source of love. (If this seems like hokum to you, follow the steps anyway – they will bring the same benefit of peace hand in hand with uplift and enlightenment.)

- ✓ Sit quietly.
- ✓ Steady your breathing, slowing it down a little and taking air deep into your lungs.
- ✓ Be aware of your body and mind relaxing and appreciate how good this feels.
- ✓ Lift up your heart to the sacred sense.
- ✓ Feel light and love radiating from it towards you as you face it.
- ✓ Let the sensation of healing, inspiring, energizing and yet at the same time relaxing positivity flow right through your being.
- ✓ Feel the joy and give thanks.

Follow the spiritual path that's right for you

Spirituality can be expressed and enjoyed in many ways. As in meditation, you may prefer to follow a guided way or to do your own thing. You may find it easier to sense your spirituality in silence or through music, in solitude or in company. You may like organized religion and that's fine too – as long as it feels right to you. Your preferences may change or adapt as you go through life. At different stages we may feel comfortable with one way, but then realize it's no longer the best way for us, only perhaps later to see the good in it and return.

There are many ways to connect with our spirituality. Providing we are careful at all costs not to impose our way on others or feel it makes us superior, whatever works for us, now, is good. The main purpose of any spiritual path is to let a sense of spiritual positivity and connection flow through us and to experience joy in our communication with the source of our being and our world.

When I was at school – a Christian school, as nearly all the schools in the United Kingdom then were – we had assembly and prayers every morning of the school term and all the year round we'd go to our own churches for Sunday services too. We pretty much knew off by heart the prayers we recited together and I rarely thought about the words, probably instead much preferring to think about our current passions such as ponies (one of mine) or boys and falling in love!

Later in life, when I'd become more spirituality aware, I loved the immediacy of the feeling of spiritual connection and communication when I prayed or meditated alone. For a time I revisited organized religion and found I immediately loved the sense of peace and holiness in the beautiful, ancient church. The warm sense of companionship was positive too. But the dogma worried me – it seemed so man-made and dictatorial – and the vicars led us through the service so fast there was barely time to keep up, let alone think about what we were saying. Was it a ritualistic social gathering masquerading as worship? For a while I felt cynical. But then it occurred to me that the prayers and hymns were much like and served the same purpose as the chanting that some religions, notably Buddhism, espouse and are good in that you are lulled into a spiritual state where you feel as though you're on a higher, spiritual plane, resonating with the love of the sacred sense.

Another – and for me preferable – way with pre-written prayers for example the Lord's Prayer in Christianity, whether praying with others or alone, is to slow down a little and think of the words you're reciting, taking in their meaning and enjoying their sublime beauty and wisdom.

I mention this not because I'm exhorting you to attend church or say prayers that someone else has written but because you may well do so already and, if so, it's good to feel enthusiastic about it and do it the way that's best and most sympathetic for you. As Jung said, a spiritual heritage you know well can be very positive in helping you find peace and transcendence.

Or perhaps for now, like me, you find yourself at a place in your life where you are or will be happiest reaching out to God directly. You'll be aware of the spiritual path throughout the day, actually making connections or just being aware of the possibility at various times. You could be alone or in company, especially that of friends who are spiritual too. You could be working, gardening or walking, swimming or enjoying another physical pastime or sport, and it often happens when you're being creative or enjoying one of the arts. It's a knowing. A feeling of infinite love. A wonderful mystery. Awesome – truly! Sometimes you'll feel you are being guided or will receive insights and understanding. It's constructive, enlightening, peace-making. It feels good. And it sends positivity through every part of you.

Appreciate the positive power of prayer

Nearly everyone has prayed. Even the most resolute atheist is likely to have at some time, as it's human nature to reach out for help beyond ourselves and other human beings. And, even if you don't believe there is anything else other than the dimensions that are proven to exist within our universe, prayer works positively in several ways other than receiving divine help. As long as you are well-intentioned and good-hearted in your prayer, it:

- ✓ Is deeply comforting.
- ✓ Feels good.
- ✓ Releases you at least temporarily from worry.

- ✓ Helps you get things in perspective.
- ✓ Helps you think things through positively.
- ✓ Relaxes you.
- ✓ Gives you courage.
- ✓ Gives a feeling of connection and support.

Though our prayers may not be granted or answered, they are healing and restorative. Prayer helps us through loss, pain, change and indecision. Prayer can be gentle and soothing or demanding and rousing. It can be quietly comforting or dazzlingly inspirational. Unless you are in dire straits and praying urgently in an emergency, beginning it with praise and thanks settles you into it.

When you are praying:

- ✓ Relax in the acceptance that you are connecting with goodness and love.
- ✓ Focus completely on your conversation.
- ✓ You may wish to ask for guidance for the best way forward and for sustenance and help along the way.
- ✓ Ask for forgiveness – for yourself and your own for others.
- ✓ Feel that you are – somewhere, somehow – heard.
- ✓ Feel the wonder of this and let your heart be full of love.

When we can't bring ourselves to ask for help for others or to forgive them, we're in danger of sinking into bitterness, resentment and even hate, all of which boomerang straight back against us, throwing our equilibrium out of kilter and sabotaging happiness. Prayer saves us from this if we simply hand over our feelings to the greater wisdom, asking it to deal with the situation and care for and guide the others involved, admitting honestly that we feel unable to. The relief is enormous.

Prayer works the same way with seemingly insoluble problems. Hand them over to God – again, even if you're not a believer, do so in your mind, imagining as you do so that you *are* being listened to and that your prayer will be attended to – and feel the weight of the burden of worry and negativity dropping away from you and dissolving. Do this whenever you've done all you can to sort things out yourself, do it before you try, do it when you can't get to sleep or you wake in the night tense with troubled thoughts. Ask for help. It will come as surely as morning follows night. I don't know how, but I do know that help comes, in some way – not always instantly, not always how we think it will, but it comes.

Do I believe in an interventionist higher power? Not in the sense that there is an intelligence manipulating us and granting our every request. After all, we have free will and the opportunity to make our own way in life and to make our own choices and decisions, so it wouldn't make sense for us to be helped every time we wished to be. But I do believe in the power of love and positivity, very much so, as I've been aware of loving protection and guidance from another dimension many times in my life. But like everyone I've had terrible times in my life too and others have asked: 'Why me – why should this happen to me?' and 'If there is a God why has He allowed this to happen?' The answers are: 'Why not me?' and 'I'm a living being – I'm liable to experience all sorts of aspects of life – that is what being alive is all about.'

We can't be happy all the time and we can't expect to go through life with no problems and no grief. There is in every long human life unavoidable unhappiness and we will have to face at some stage the death of some loved ones and, when the time comes, our own death. But we can always hold on to our positivity and, though prayer may not save us from danger, hurt, trauma or tragedy, it always helps us bear it.

Prayer allows us to find peace and equilibrium even in the midst of great difficulty. It is extraordinarily sustaining and positive.

It even helps us lose the fear of death and face it positively – but more on this in Chapter 7.

Perhaps our prayers are heard by something beyond our world, but certainly they open our minds and subconscious to find positive ways forward ourselves from our inner wisdom. I think it's a mixture of both.

One way or another, as the writer Ruth Gledhill observed, although we may not believe in God, the fact is prayer works.

Meditate the way that's right for you

Meditation is an essential part of most forms of yoga and shares the same meanings of union and contemplation. It's a way of connecting with your inner self and, if you wish, the wisdom of the universe and the sacred sense in an emotional, mental and physical oasis of peace and stillness.

There are many ways to meditate and if you are already comfortable with your own that's fine; if not you can find the one (or more) that is right for you by trying the different ways to see which is your best meditation 'home'.

That's an apt word as when we meditate it does feel like coming home. Sometimes I'll let days or even weeks go by, forgetting or wilfully not making time to meditate, and then when I get back into the practice again it's a wonderful feeling of being welcomed and I always think: 'I must do this regularly as it's so good.'

Many people like to meditate while using physical postures and positions to settle, quiet and focus the mind on peace and stillness. Hatha Yoga, Pilates and Tai Chi are well-known forms of this. Particularly popular with the people I meditate with is a practice where you sit quietly and focus your attention on every part of your body, starting at the tips of your toes and working upwards to the top of your head. We then breathe deeply and slowly for a few minutes, doing nothing but noticing the breath as you draw it in to yourself and let it out. This is followed by a quiet time where we are at peace – no worrying, no thinking, just peaceful.

I like that way of meditating very much, but I'm also often drawn to the way of sitting quietly in silence and 'listening'. Sometimes it is a quiet contemplative time or sometimes I intuit something that is like a message or revelation. Always I feel completely safe – as though I'm being gently protected and looked after. Always, even in troubled times, I feel stronger, balanced, calmer and altogether better by the end of the meditation. If ever I happen to be worrying about something, even a few minutes of this kind of meditation is like a healing balm.

Another way which can feel blissful is, once settled into the peace of meditation, to feel that love is flowing through you. Feel it – drink it in – and imagine you are sending it to someone or some people you love, or to the living world and the sacred sense beyond.

Another common form of meditation is to use the oasis of peace to think and reason deeply, searching for the right way, truth and profundity. I find that a good time for this is when I wake at night or first thing in the morning. In the stillness and quiet I can ask myself to be absolutely honest in whether I have an issue that's bothering me, or a decision that needs to be made and am addressing it in perspective and clarity with a positive and loving attitude. Often it's reassuring that all is well with my take on the situation. But quite often I realize I've got the situation a bit off kilter and by righting it, the way ahead is cleared and I am soothed and understand the best approach or way of dealing with it.

Another way is meditation on the move. I know people who meditate when skiing, running or sailing or, like me, going for long walks. I usually take the dog with me, and it's also good on your own or with like-minded friends. As you settle into the rhythm of the exercise your breathing steadies too and your mind is free to follow the path of contemplation or perhaps another of the ways above.

When you meditate:

- ▶ Remember there is no 'right' or 'wrong' way. The way that allows you to settle down quietly and feel at peace is your way and it is good.
- ▶ If unwanted thoughts or worries disturb your peace, simply let them go. Unless you want to focus on one, as in the fourth way above, just say to yourself 'Not now – I'll think about that later' and it will leave your mind there and then.
- ▶ If you have judgmental feelings about someone, send them love instead.
- ▶ Breathe deeply and slowly.
- ▶ Let every muscle and tension relax.
- ▶ Be entirely in the moment.
- ▶ Feel the energy of love and positivity, peace and calm in you and around you.

People meditating often find that they drop off to sleep especially in their first few meditations. I did quite recently when listening to a recorded visualization. Someone told me later that this is called 'tripping out', which made me chuckle. So if you do sleep, enjoy the trip and feel the vibe of refreshment and restoration when you awake! If you'd rather not sleep because you want the deeper relaxation and the wonderful feeling of connection of meditation, a good position is to sit cross-legged with your back straight. Even the most un-agile of us can sit cross-legged if we sit on a good thick cushion or better still a church kneeling pad – you can buy them at church supply shops and online.

Meditation is a delight and can be an experience of profound truth and enlightenment. Do not suppose, as some would have you believe, that for this you'd have to do it for years and attain 'perfection'. You may experience spiritual bliss – you may meet God – at any time.

On a more prosaic note, medical doctors and other scientists know that research has shown meditation to be a deeper form of relaxation than sleep. My friends and I know that positivity flows when we meditate and we feel washed with a healing balm. I can't recommend it highly enough!

Practise the magic of praise and spiritual wonder

The mystery of life. Just thinking of spirituality this way feels good – it's exciting, full of wonder, mystical. It explains, too, something of the deep inner knowledge we have of a God of love and an essential goodness that all the main religions relate to. It's mankind that has, for various cultural purposes over the years, written dogma around spirituality that incites nations to fight, supposedly in its name, and even sets neighbour against neighbour. Get back to the basic teaching and it is to love others and treat them well.

With our personal spirituality, we can reach out directly to the life-giving, love-giving source of our world and our being, and then we can feel from our hearts the wonder of being able to communicate. This is a mystery in itself, for we don't know how the connection is made – we only know we can make it. It's easy to forget how breath-taking this ability is and to become complacent. It's great to be able to connect with our spirituality at any time whenever we wish to through thought, prayer and meditation, and the feeling of positivity we get from this is palpable, but take time at least now and then to register how precious this sense is, to wonder at it, praise it and give thanks. When you do you'll feel your spirit and your inner positive energy shining within and from you.

Hymns do it for us easily and joyously. When we sing our hearts out in a stream of beautiful praise set to a melody that uplifts us or moves us deeply, we're filled with love that seems to transcend everything we know on this earth and reach another spiritual dimension.

Even on a day that's emotionally grey, when you sing praise to the highest heights you can imagine you'll let positivity back in, giving you hope and enabling you to think constructively how to weather the storm and if possible improve the situation.

I like sometimes – especially when outside in a beautiful place, for instance, a park, beside the sea or a river, up a hill enjoying a great view or in the majesty of a forest – to stretch my arms up and say (aloud if there's no one about, silently in my mind if there is) THANK YOU, and sense the cry of thanks going around this world we know and slipping through the portals we haven't yet mapped to the dimension beyond and the maker of our universe. Whatever problems we may be facing, even when some might think we've precious little to be thankful for right now, doing this feels good, and leaves you feeling better afterwards too. It's a spiritual tonic of positive energy that is healing and revitalizing.

Try it for yourself now and whenever you have a few moments to yourself:

- ✓ Stretch – feel your muscles tense.
- ✓ Relax – but stay aware of the alertness of your whole body.
- ✓ Give thanks for your body and your life.
- ✓ Say thank you, too, for the love you give out and the way you are loved.
- ✓ Praise the world you live in and the sacred sense in any words that feel right. For instance, I sometimes say (out loud if alone or in my mind) 'You are wonderful – I love you!'
- ✓ Feel your connection with and love for the sacred sense with all your mind, heart and soul. Feel it well up and, with your spirit, soar.
- ✓ Give thanks and praise for anyone or anything that you are especially glad about in your life right now.
- ✓ Take time just to feel the sense of peace and perhaps joy you have.

Find joy in the sacred

Places, people, the arts – all these can give a sense of having been blessed by a shining spirituality, something other, something so good and pure that it's beyond our comprehension but we know it and resonate with it. We may recognize holiness in someone who leads a simple and down to earth life and in everyday things too.

We've already looked at the sense you may get in a place where suddenly you're transfixed by the holiness of it – I mentioned the time in the garden when I was healed and refreshed and given strength. The same kind of feeling may strike you when you look at or touch something that's has a special significance to you spiritually. When it happens:

- ✓ Linger for a few minutes at least to concentrate on it.
- ✓ Sense the sacredness of it purifying and healing you.
- ✓ Let the wonder and feeling of belonging you're experiencing energize and inspire you.
- ✓ Feel the peace of it, the timelessness.

I have been thinking of the people or things in my life that I've felt are sacred and who or which take me straight to a spiritual sense:

- ▶ A friend, Daisy, whom I met when she was elderly and knew for her remaining years. She was a Cockney and characteristically down to earth and outspoken, but she was a good person through and through. I always left her company feeling I'd been graced because though she wasn't religious at all, I somehow knew she was very, very close to and beloved by God.
- ▶ Certain paintings, such as those by Claude Monet, William Turner and the later ones by W. de Kooning.
- ▶ A sculpture by Elizabeth Bradley of one of the sacrificial Inca children, which shimmers with holiness and never fails to remind me that I and every one of us bear some responsibility for the ills that man has done and continues to do but perhaps can atone for it – somehow – by doing our best to guard against evil and spread the word of love and kindness, goodness and truth.
- ▶ A little sculpture of an angel by the artist Linda Sébéo Cohu – that touched me with its sacredness the first time I saw it and does every time I look at it.
- ▶ Angels generally! These mythical beings are perhaps the most universal and beloved of all the symbols of sacredness, for they remind us of the blessing of our spirituality and the innate feeling that we are protected, no matter what happens to us, and loved.

- ▶ Books that have blessed my life. Mister God, This is Anna by Fynn and Pilgrims: Two Unlikely Friends Unravel the Mystery of Life by Paul McDermott spring to mind first – these are gems. Several books by Paul Gallico that I read years ago worked a kind of spiritual magic for me; so did Surprised by Joy by C.S. Lewis. Books with a truth and simplicity so positive it seems to shine from them and through you. Then there are the timeless classics The Prophet by Kahlil Gibran and God Calling by Two Listeners.
- ▶ Poems too – so many.

Think about times when something touches *you* spiritually. Write them down and if you like add your thoughts about them in a book, along with favourite poems perhaps; you can then pick it up whenever you need an uplift or just want to experience a moment of sanctity.

Understand the presence of heaven on earth

Heaven as a concept of a nirvana we go to after death – the home of God and the angels – is another myth, and a very beautiful one that many believe is a reality and of course may be. However, heaven as a blissful spiritual experience or way of living is definitely real and we can each enjoy it here on earth in our daily lives.

It's a way of positive being that can range from inner contentment to happiness and joy. It can be an ephemeral experience or last for long passages of time in the different stages of our lives. Perhaps it is a current of energy that flows through our lives, at times showing up for us palpably, at other times of loss and distress flowing quietly beneath our consciousness, ready to bring us delight again when we have healed.

It's here with you now. Not something that happens to you, not dependent on the purchase of some thing, no matter how necessary or desirable that thing may seem.

Heaven is an attitude and a state of being that lives within us whenever we seek it and have a willingness to recognize it and experience it. It's a feeling of being spiritually at one with the greater consciousness, a readiness to feel the moments or stretches of peace or contentment, joy, happiness, love, or affection we are blessed with within an overall feeling of well-being.

It isn't necessarily dependent on things going right but is there for us in all kinds of circumstance. Our inner sense of heaven can survive even the horrors of war or other forms of man's inhumanity to man.

Sometimes it's a case of hanging on to small incidents of grace that create for us an oasis, a retreat from troubles or sorrow. Sometimes it's a feeling of your hand being held.

I've just read that we are guided every moment and if we only stop to sense the best way, the right decision will come to us. Whether this is spiritual guidance or contacting our own common sense, I know it's true, but how easy it is to forget to do it, or to stubbornly cling to our procrastination, indecision or confusion. Asking for guidance in a spiritual sense is always a good idea, to help to get through the walls we build to make things difficult for ourselves, or to stop us putting them up in the first place. It's so easy, too – a few simple steps:

- ✓ Pause in your ruminating.
- ✓ Clear your mind of the constant switching between options.
- ✓ Establish the feeling you have a spiritual connection to guidance.
- ✓ Listen.
- ✓ Be aware of the right thing to do.
- ✓ Write it down.

The last step is useful, and it's vital whenever good ideas come to us, especially at night. Then especially it seems so blindingly clear that you think you'll never forget the revelation, but a minute's distraction or a nice long sleep and it's gone, perhaps for ever. So get into the habit of writing down thoughts and ideas, especially on the spiritual front, as any breakthroughs in understanding are precious and a great help in letting positive energy flow smoothly and sweetly. The more you practise connecting and listening and following the right way for you that you sense in the deepest part of your being and truth, the easier and better life will be and the more you will be living in a feel-good state of positivity and grace.

Show up, be present and live in the moment

Life is too short, too precious to be spiritually lazy. Whether you *believe* in your spirituality, or religion or the existence of anything else other than this world is irrelevant to this – you are a living creature with a good brain, an extraordinary amount of intelligence, a unique personality. You are loving and lovable. Above all, you have consciousness of all this.

So be aware – 100 per cent aware – of your presence in this amazing world. You are a piece of the jigsaw, a part of the mystery. You have been given the gift of life that no one understands, not even the greatest brains in the world.

Take an interest in the luminescence, the numinous wonder of your presence here, at this moment and for your whole lifetime.

A friend who I've often meditated with put it this way:

'Presence – just being, this moment, this minute, is a powerful feeling. For me it's most noticeable in times of quiet. I try to feel this sense of now at least once a day. It can be anywhere, though places of beauty help me tune in. The most important thing is just to stop your thoughts and focus entirely on this moment.

'It's a deep feeling of oneness with the world and that I'm meant to be here, everything is somehow right. It always calms me and helps me, even when my life is troubled. It often uplifts me so I feel like smiling or even dancing for joy!'

These moments of peace, healing and sometimes rapture are gifts of inestimable value that you can opt to receive, enjoy and value any day or every day. Take a few moments for yourself. At first as you practise this it may seem that nothing happens. But in time the magic of deep peace will come easily to you. It's a small miracle.

You are a miracle. This world and universe is too.

What lies behind it, beneath it, around it, throughout it?

Never cease the willingness to connect and engage and appreciate with all your being the gift of your spirituality.

It's a light to lighten your path, a beacon of hope and joy. The essence of our 'knowing' glows within each of us and our spirituality is there for us to find and cherish if we wish to. When we do so, it bursts into life – positive, enriching and life-enhancing.

7

....

Health and healing

In this chapter, you'll embrace positivity when you:
- *Find and live by your best personal health recipe to live vibrantly incorporating the fundamentals of good food, rest and exercise*
- *Harmonize mind, body and soul for optimum well-being*
- *Deal positively with physical pain and disability, and with mental illness including low spirits, anxiety and apathy*
- *Use your natural healing ability for yourself and others*
- *Accept the ageing process and even enjoy it!*

A positive approach to health maximizes our energy and helps realize our full potential for a wonderful zest for life. When you feel the best you can physically, you give your mind and spirit a great base from which to flourish too. Positive thinking gives us the power to optimize our health and healing and feel good physically *and* mentally.

Live vibrantly

The human body is a miracle. We each have around 100 trillion cells, each one a living thing, and through them our bodies are constantly replenishing and renewing giving us our well-being, vitality and individuality.

Your whole system is healing itself all the time, in body, mind and spirit. Life is positive and powerful. It wants us to be fit, to feel good, to have the energy not just to survive but to enjoy being in this amazing world in which we find ourselves. Certainly, genetic problems we're born with are unavoidable and unexpected illness is a matter of chance too. But we can still look after ourselves and our loved ones, doing whatever we can to help homoeostasis – the body's natural healing dynamic – and enable well-being.

Vibrant health is our natural state of being and an on-going process. Whatever type of body we have, we can look after it as best we can, right through our lives. This means that whatever the state of your health now, you can resume, maintain or step up this self-healing and self-optimization. In many ways there's never been a time more conducive to living healthily. We have a good choice of food. Our health care services are superb. We have ample opportunity to exercise not just our bodies but our minds too.

The most exciting thing is that our all-round well-being is very much down to us – it's our own choice to live well, consciously and capably looking after our health. When we do it's fascinating – rather like following the course of our own personal detective story. The science of nutrition for instance, is complex; the more you learn, the more there is to learn and it's entirely up to you how far you take your knowledge. It's the same with physiology and medicine, and exercise, energy and metabolism. Then there's the whole picture of mental and emotional health you could spend your lifetime becoming an expert on any one aspect and that, of course, is just what the specialists of the medical world do.

Thankfully unless it's your metier you don't have to go all the way with your interest. For all-round good health – that's feeling good, feeling full of vitality, on-going healing as your cells regenerate and your energy replenishes – all you have to do is take a holistic, positive interest. It feels good to do this and it's fascinating and straightforward.

When we look after our health and more than that, cherish it, it's a big part of loving ourselves too. This has a knock-on effect on our confidence, self-esteem, general outlook and all-round positivity. We don't have to be fanatical and over-do it – just be caring and positive.

The fundamentals of physical health are good food, sound sleep and exercise. You probably know about these, so I'll just run through them quickly.

FOOD THAT'S GOOD FOR YOU

As a general maxim, include a feel-good balance of the following:

▶ Fruit
▶ Leafy green vegetables and salads
▶ Natural (i.e. unsalted and unroasted) nuts and seeds

- ▶ Whole carbohydrates such as pulses, potatoes and wholemeal bread
- ▶ High-protein food such as eggs, yoghurt, cheese, and pulses, but go easy on meat and poultry as it takes more time and energy to digest
- ▶ Olive oil or sunflower oil. The first is delicious, the second pretty much tasteless, so both go well with raw and cooked food. Unlike saturated fat, they won't clog up your arteries – they'll help blood circulation instead. As part of a salad dressing or home-made mayonnaise they're an easy addition to a good-for-you diet.
- ▶ Plenty of fluids. Water is the best. It's so easy to forget but we should aim to drink at least 2 litres a day and obviously if you're doing a lot of aerobic exercise you'll need more.

Do buy organic foods as much as possible to save your body having to cope with the effects of chemicals used in production. Only ever buy meat and poultry from animals that have been reared well and as naturally as possible. Buying broiler chicken and any other kind of intensively farmed meat is out, for how can we expect to feel good about ourselves and therefore our health if we tacitly accept cruelty?

SLEEP WELL

When you wake after a good night's sleep you feel as though you've been washed pure and blessed with rest and relaxation. It's thought to be an important part of our physiological health too as it helps the growth and maintenance of the body's immune, nervous, skeletal and muscular systems. Our brains in particular need regular, sound sleep to stay bright and efficient. Although occasional sleep deprivation doesn't seem to be harmful, most people feel they function better generally when they've slept well, especially if they slept for their own optimum time.

Here are my tips for sleeping well:

- ▶ Often the reason for insomnia is going to bed too early or getting up too late. Don't lie in bed much longer than the time you want to sleep. For example, if you ideally like to have 8 hours' sleep but like, for example, to read for half an hour or so before you go off to sleep, go to bed at 10.30 pm and set the alarm for 7 am. Whether or not you've slept well, or even at all, get up when the alarm sounds. Within a few days you'll have established a new sound sleep pattern as your body and mind will have realized they've only got a certain number of hours to sleep and will use it. This really works.

▸ Free your mind from night-time worry by meditating during the evening. The relaxation is a different kind from sleep and very deep, and it gives a certain kind of inner peace which encourages good sleep once you go to bed. If you do wake in the night or too early in the morning, clear your mind of nagging thoughts which put you on alert by meditating or praying.

▸ Tell yourself, as you go off to sleep, that you will sleep for the desired number of hours and wake at the time you wish to get up, rested and at peace.

You may find sleep lets your mind reach parts of your subconscious you can't always access during waking! Often when I awake I remember something I was trying to recall the day before, or find I have the answer to a question or puzzle that I've been fretting over. Sometimes there'll be a nudge about something that needs doing that hadn't occurred to me before. Creatively it's a boon too; I may wake up with an idea or inspiration for my painting or writing or an insight that's helpful for another aspect of my life.

Keeping a notebook by your bed is a boon for jotting down anything that occurs to you when you newly emerge from sleep, as though you'll think you won't forget it, you probably will as soon as you're fully awake. Writing in a stream of consciousness for two or three pages is a brilliant way to start the day too. You feel so full of zest afterwards and it's surprising how often an intriguing thought, good idea or even fully fledged poem will find itself among the words that flow on to the paper.

EXERCISE

We each need to discover the kind and amount of exercise that suits us individually. It's essential for the body's suppleness and fitness, helping our metabolism and blood circulation system work well too. Exercise is also about the positive, vibrant feelings that come with it.

It feels good to be in control as you choose the kind of exercise you like and how often you do it.

Exercise releases feel-good chemicals as we're doing it, and as our blood flows faster the oxygen makes us feel more alert and upbeat too.

Outdoor exercise is particularly beneficial because it gets us out in the daylight which is naturally uplifting. Doctors often suggest walking and swimming as being the most useful all-round exercise as they don't cause a lot of wear and tear on our bodies and are good for circulation.

You don't have to be a fitness fanatic – in fact it's probably best for your body that you're not, as, like most things, unless you're an athlete exercise is usually most beneficial in moderation.

Choose something that you thoroughly enjoy, physically, mentally and if possible sensually too, and you'll get even more positivity from it. This kind of super-feel-good exercise keeps your personal power recharged right throughout the day long after the chemical high of the exercise itself has faded.

Exercising alone and in company each has its own specific benefits. In solitude, it gives you the chance to meditate and think, or simply enjoy what you're doing and your surroundings. Being sociable is fun and emotionally enriching and of course conversation can be invigorating too.

I loved a counselling client's experience of swimming, which shows how just how good exercise can be for our mind, body and soul's positivity. She showed me a passage she'd written about it in her journal: 'I've started swimming regularly, sometimes on my own and sometimes with a friend, from a rocky cove on the Dorset coast. I love the feel of the water on my skin and the sensation of my whole body being supported. It feels very safe – like being carried. On a calm day, I'll float on my back and my problems seem to float off me and out to sea. Yesterday a man and his dog came swimming round the headland into the bay and we said Hi and passed the time of day. I said 'Isn't this just heaven?' and he said, 'Yes – it really is amazing,' and so there was this lovely feeling of sharing the joy too. I even like the shock of the cold water when I first go in, and when I get dry and change afterwards it feels like being a kid again.'

I said to her: 'Going swimming is making a difference to your whole sense of well-being, isn't it?'

'Yes,' she said. 'You feel so 'in the moment'. It gets everything into perspective for me and even though I can't make all my problems go away, they don't seem nearly as bad any more, I know I can cope. It's made me feel very alive, very vibrant, for the first time for years. It's probably only a very small joy – after all, it's only going swimming! – but I really feel it's turned the lights on for me in my whole life and I've turned the corner, out of depression. If this is what positivity feels like, I'm never going back round that corner again.'

I don't think swimming is a small joy. I think it's been a huge one and a very positive powerful catalyst not just in her recovery from depression, but in showing her that she is in control of her own life and can choose to be positive on an on-going basis.

Finding some form of exercise that we love, and noticing and appreciating the physical and mental benefits it gives us, can have a wonderfully positive effect on life for each of us too.

Listen to your body

We're all different in our likes and dislikes and various sensitivities, this is where my notion of the quest for good health being a detective story comes in. Knowing your own body makes sense, as no one else, not even the best informed and most empathic doctor in the world, can actually feel what you're feeling. You are the best possible witness.

For instance, take an interest in food and the bearing it has on how you are. As fuel, the food we eat has a lot to do with our health. So as an everyday practice, without getting obsessed about it, pay attention to what you're eating and any good or adverse effects of certain foods or food combinations.

Many people claim it's best not to mix carbohydrates and proteins for example and are more comfortable when they don't, but they happen to work fine together for me. On the other hand it took me a few weeks to realize that eating fruit after a meal was the cause of the indigestion I'd been experiencing. My digestion is usually trouble-free but in an effort to meet the five portions of fruit and vegetables guideline, I'd started having fruit with my meals instead of as a snack on its own, not realizing that because it's more quickly digested than most other foods, it was causing a problem.

Just as your digestion is a good indicator of whether you're eating a diet that suits you, so is your skin. One common cause of spots that we can take control of easily is too much sugar and saturated fat. Cut down drastically on chips, crisps and other foods fried in saturated fat; also regard cakes, biscuits and, sadly, chocolate and sweets, as occasional treats only and you'll probably find your skin is really grateful and soon clears. Hormone surges can also cause troubled complexions, and while the doctor can help with this, so can eating plenty of salads and green vegetables and, again, cutting right down on the sugars and fats mentioned above. One of the great pluses of growing older is that our hormones settle down and our skin improves. But if I get complacent and binge on something with a high sugar content it still has a quick adverse effect!

Taking an interest in the adage 'We are what we eat' is very positive, for it's true that when we feed ourselves with food that's good for us it feels great physically. As our brains and whole neurological system are made up of cells that are sustained and kept in top form by our food, it's vital for them.

Because eating well is a part of tender loving care, it's very positive for us psychologically too. The rest provided by good sleep also, again holistically, helps replenish and renew every part of us.

Exercise that suits us physically, mentally and even spiritually too, plays another vital part in our well-being and positivity.

It's all about paying attention to our health with a positive attitude. When something goes wrong, whether it's with the workings of our body or mind, it nags away until we pay attention to it and do whatever it takes to mend and restore our health. It makes much more sense to look after every bit of that well-ness, physically *and* psychologically when we're well.

It's easy to 'listen' to our bodies – to be aware of what we need from day to day. Yes I know your body might say, like a child, 'Chocolate! Cake! Pastry! Chips! Sugary soft drinks!' – just because we're adults doesn't mean we only crave what's good for us. But if you listen to those yearnings for fat and sugar and say, well OK, occasionally as a treat – and then listen again to what you'd really like for your feel-good health – you'll quickly find you become drawn to the healthy option food groups above most of the time and want the high-calorie 'empty' options less and less.

When we listen to what we really need, we pre-empt and often preclude issues with our digestion and the attention to our well-being greatly contributes to our all-round health.

Like most things – even inanimate ones like engines – we work best and look best when we're well cared for. It empowers us so we're firing on all cylinders. All care takes is a bit of thought – and remembering to do it. So simple, really, and caring and being cared for feels so good and very positive.

Optimize well-being

Is there such a thing as a positive attitude to health? Very much so – it's really the whole basis of well-being. It includes having confidence in yourself to look after your health as best as possible but also about forgiving yourself for not always doing so. It's about knowing yourself and getting to know your best ways to become or stay healthy. It's about having integrity in the way you live and understanding other people as best you can, but not martyring yourself to those who worry you or pull you down. All these aspects of the way you choose to live enable an equanimity that not only feels good but helps keep your self-healing power running smoothly. Other keys to it, all covered in this book and all having a direct effect on our health, are:

- ▶ Contentment with the simple things of life
- ▶ Knowing yourself and being true to yourself
- ▶ Knowing how to manage stress and bring in peace at will
- ▶ Feeling the joy of life, despite unavoidable health problems
- ▶ Feeling our healing power pulsing through us
- ▶ Appreciating our whole being: body, mind and soul
- ▶ Loving life, whatever it brings us, whatever path we follow
- ▶ Loving others and caring for them as well as ourselves.

It's a completely holistic state of harmony where everything dovetails in an extraordinarily symbiotic working model. In harmonizing all the aspects of our well-being we naturally give thanks for our health and take our place gladly in the similarly self-sustaining, self-healing eco-system of our wonderfully colourful, cosmopolitan planet.

Good health, well-being, *joie-de-vivre*. The words shine as you read, write or speak them and of course they all feel great to experience. Yet a lot of the time, unless there's a problem, we don't think much if at all about how we are. We mosey along in the busy-ness of everyday life scarcely appreciating how well we are and only noticing our health when something goes out of kilter and we feel unwell. Just think what an opportunity there is to be glad, to focus on the fact that yes, actually, we don't just feel OK, we really do feel very good. Noticing it gives you a spring and a sparkle and ups your positive energy level in the process.

How sad when someone asks another 'How are you?' and, despite being in essentially good health, they answer: 'Not so bad,' or something self-deprecating like: 'Oh, you know, muddling along.' You can see as well as hear them repressing their natural health with this grey monotone.

How different and good it is to hear – and see – a glad, fully meant, response: 'I'm fine thank you – how about you?' You're both uplifted in the exchange of positive energy.

When we're not well, it's a different thing altogether, but we can still be positive. In fact we have three positive choices: if we know what the problem is we can say cheerfully we're 'fine' to save worrying the other person for now, or because it isn't appropriate to tell them the problem. Or, if we feel out of sorts one way or another but don't know why, we can say we're 'fine' and determine to find out what's wrong and do something about it, seeing a doctor if necessary. Or we can choose to be open and say 'Actually not so good' and explain what's wrong in as much or little detail as we wish. We help our homoeostasis – the way our whole system works to restore and maintain our healthy all-round balance – by noticing any health issues, reviewing them and taking constructive action, rather than denying their existence to ourselves.

Honesty about and attention to health doesn't mean moaning and moping though. There are always blessings to count, and when we do, we always feel better. Positivity is healing in all ways, mentally and emotionally as well as physically, and when we encourage it and let ourselves feel it fully, we activate our own power to enjoy life as best we possibly can, even if our health is presently damaged, but more of this in the next section.

Deal with poor health positively

Thinking and living positively is our choice in health even when we're not well. It transcends pain and disability, lifts our spirits and helps us relax and deal with worries constructively.

Even in severe chronic illness or disability we can continue to shine and enjoy life. When we do, it lights up those around us, not just ourselves. With everyone feeling better, not just ourselves, the whole atmosphere around us changes and life is good despite pain and despite, in worst scenarios, lack of hope of recovery.

Think for a moment of Professor Stephen Hawking. With his level of disability, few would have imagined that he could live as vibrantly as he does, using his brilliant mind to further science and reaching out to us all with clear, beautiful prose. Think of countless military personnel who lose limbs but go on so courageously to live full lives.

And I'm thinking of the teenager I met with her family on a train recently as mentioned earlier. She had quite severe learning difficulties and was noisy and boisterous but delightfully happy in her exuberance. Instead of trying to suppress her natural vitality, her mother, aunt and sisters laughed and sang with her, and I did too, affected by their love and high spirits. They were infinitely patient, infinitely positive, and this increased their rapport and happiness where it could so easily have been sabotaged by regret, impatience and frustration, which in turn would have upset the teenager and made things more difficult.

All these examples show how good life can be in potentially hugely adverse circumstances if we choose a positive attitude and make the best of what we do have, working with it and refusing to be pulled down.

It's the same with pain.

Jacky, a friend of mine who has had a fair share of health problems, doesn't moan about them. She either encourages her body to recover as quickly as possible or, for anything chronic, bounces along positively anyway, counting her blessings generally. She says health is 'an intelligent attitude to life' which, although it doesn't make us escape pain, influences how we keep going in the present and into the future.

Helen, a trained nurse who had to give up her career because of an illness that means she is in constant pain, also refuses to be mentally bowed by her misfortune. She loves people and is great company. She has a wonderful smile and once I asked her how she managed to stay so cheerful despite the pain. She answered: 'Nobody wants to know you if you're miserable. Anyway, I don't do pathetic!'

Bob, her husband, told me: 'Helen always puts on a front of being cheerful – half the time people don't know there's a problem. Everyone loves being around her and that's great for her as she loves their company too.'

Her family, friends and just about everyone she comes into contact with respond in kind to her infectious warmth, sense of humour, evident enjoyment of life and kindness, and that in turn makes her happy. It's a cycle of positivity that pain cannot spoil.

'Ah, but what about depression and anxiety?' a fellow therapist asked. 'When you're severely, clinically depressed you can't even think straight half the time, let alone think positively!' Acute and chronic illness may certainly need medical attention and I always advise checking out any symptoms and problems with the doctor. But I believe that no matter how bad our condition, we can usually, somehow, utilize the power of positivity. It is there and we have the choice to be aware of it and use it.

However tiny the positive step, we can take it. Always it makes a difference in some way, even if that's presently obscured from us. Our positive energy wants to help us and wants to be used by us. All we have to do is be open to it and allow it to start helping us. In turn our natural immune system and other healing powers will start to kick in. In health, never say 'I'm never going to get better,' or 'I can't help myself.' Even when physically nothing more can be done, there is always the possibility of calming or strengthening emotionally and, in feeling better, we usually find we can cope better with illness and pain and, in conjunction with the medical team, learn to manage it and use pain relief as appropriate.

With depression, sometimes that first step is to get help from someone who will help us take the next ones and set ourselves back on a positive path. When we're depressed it's like being in a muddy pool. We may know what it's all about, but can't see a viable way out or decide which is best, and go round and round looking for the way forward, constantly reviewing the options.

A client who came to me for counselling help had been in this position. Despite being a normally positive person, she too had been stuck. For her it felt like wading in mud and not being able to get out. A very good friend of hers had realized that just listening over and over again wasn't helping her and said, 'There's something behind this, Lyn, and you need to deal with it. Find a counsellor. Not next week, not tomorrow – right now when you put down the phone.'

In her heart Lyn knew she was right, and when she contacted me on the phone she felt she could talk to me and work with me. Her friend was right, there were issues from way back that, despite her common sense and general positive attitude, were stopping her from dealing with her present and finding the right path to move on freely. In time she fathomed and faced them, and then was able to leave the negativity surrounding them in the past where it belonged and live fully and positively in the present again, no longer dragged back by them.

It took a lot of courage and that in itself boosted her self-confidence. The whole process re-engaged her with the joy of living in the moment and also gave her the tools to keep her positive energy flowing freely whatever challenges of life she may face in the future.

Positivity + healing = personal energy + happiness. But the current vogue for purely cognitive behaviour solutions isn't always enough in itself to fulfil this. To follow the practical route out of depression we very often need a holistic approach, as Lyn's friend sensed and she herself recognized.

Living the joy of life is based on our being aware of all aspects of our health, mind body and soul, listening to them, being guided by them, and seeking guidance when we need to.

When we've experienced depression and recovered from it, we can look back and see we've learned a lot about ourselves and about the nature of our depression. We can also reflect on what led up to it. Self-understanding and an understanding of our emotional history can help tremendously in finding and staying on the positive path of well-being. In remembering how the cycle of depression first began, we can notice any similar changes that happen again and instead of them leading us back into depression, be aware of what's happening or might happen and take positive steps to stop it doing so. Counselling can be extremely therapeutic at this early stage in preventing depression from getting a grip. Or you may see that you can adjust certain aspects of your life to stave off stress-inducing pressure.

Terence, a psychotherapist who specializes in helping clients avoid or recover from depression, told me: 'When people take an interest in the potential causes of depression and any pattern they've previously experienced, they're already half way to preventing it in the first place or recovering quickly.'

Taking an interest in a positive lifestyle is hugely helpful too. 'If only everyone would learn the many ways to live positively and realize that they can deliberately choose to make them a regular part of their life, most forms of depression would become obsolete.'

I asked him if he believed everyone could learn to live positively.

'Absolutely. It's simply an approach to life. Can we choose it? Very much so.'

The first course of action must be to consult your doctor, who can assess whether anti-depressants or counselling is advisable. However, most doctors agree that, except in severe depression, self-understanding with a positive cognitive approach works very well in aiding natural healing and many consider it a vital adjunct to anti-depressants.

We can all support our mental health by treasuring our brains, which store all the information about our abilities and enables us to recognize and use them. Your brain is of inestimable value and in looking after your personal mix of intelligence you simultaneously keep your brain fit. When we look after our minds this way we walk tall, feel bright and well, and boost our self-esteem too.

Thought, conversation and other forms of communication, specific mental exercise like work, puzzles, games that make you think and use logic, questioning, debate – these are just some of the things that keep our minds alert and our brains at peak fitness. As well as exercise, a good diet, rest and relaxation are as important to the brain as they are to other parts of the body.

Encouragement helps our brains too. Constantly bashing ourselves with self-deprecating remarks like: 'I'm really thick' or allowing loved ones to say things like 'You're so stupid' can convince the brain, if it hears it enough times, to doubt its natural ability and even go into a kind of slow motion. Inspire ourselves and each other on the other hand, appreciating our various forms of intelligence, abilities and talents, and our brains are infected by the enthusiasm and positivity and work even better. Praise and encouragement are wonderful food for the mind.

Often of course, criticism may be relevant and valuable and changes advisable. Then, if we keep it constructive and look for any good we can, so that we don't make our brains feel we're blaming or shaming them, it too is good food for the mind and hones our intelligence and our work.

Wholeheartedly, mindfully and with spirit we can give ourselves holistic healing and well-being as a way of life that lifts us up and carries us along. It's surprisingly easy – all we have to do is give it a try. When we do it happens. Sometimes passively, sometimes actively, but always very positively, you feel better. You feel, quite simply, good.

Delight in your own mood-altering ability

Your brain is as incredibly complex as it is precious. It's a computer, if you like, far more intelligent than anything we have ever managed to create. Although robust in many ways, it's also extremely sensitive and finely tuned. And it's an important source of your positive thinking ability and the positive power this releases.

Don't risk damaging it with recreational drugs. Avoid completely any known to be potentially addictive the first time you use it, for instance crack cocaine and heroin. Also avoid completely those like hashish and Ecstasy that, while they seem to be harmless to many, have been known to cause brain damage in some people.

Question the fact that it's become somehow cool to get drunk out of our minds. Out of your mind? Happiness and positive energy only flow through you steadily and surely when you are *in* your mind and engaged with it! Stoned, the high is brief and the natural, healthy stasis of your mind may struggle to rebalance itself.

Yet when you use your positivity, in any of the myriad ways that you choose, to feel good and sometimes delightfully upbeat, the feeling is not just pleasant but long lasting. Unlike a chemical high, the feeling doesn't need more and more of a potentially dangerous substance to recreate it. We can feel great from our own positivity virtually any time we choose, and the more we do, the easier it is.

Cathy, 22, told me: 'I used to do drugs, lots of them, but I got worried about it because several of our crowd started suffering from depression, and I finally stopped taking anything when one of them had a complete breakdown.

'To be honest, because I'd been lucky enough not to have become addicted, and also because lately, however much more I took, the high I'd been getting hadn't been nearly as good as it originally was, it wasn't difficult for me to give up.

'The silly thing – or rather the great thing – is that I have such a good time now when I go out with friends or just have fun with the family at home. Laughter and bopping, even good conversation can do it for me just as well as the drugs ever did, even in the beginning.'

Cathy's right: except as medication in illness, we don't need mood-enhancing chemicals. We can feel good and be content as a general way of being and at times be truly joyous all by our own volition.

Positivity is an approach to life that feels good in itself and releases a powerful kind of energy that helps us dispel stress and negative moods. It allows us to notice all the good things to enjoy about life, and also enables us to do just that – enjoy them wholeheartedly.

Laughter, love and creativity, for example, all make us feel wonderful – and are safe, easy and a sheer delight to experience.

Use your natural healing ability

Our immune systems work best when we're positive. An upbeat attitude directly helps our natural immunity make the most of the health we have, heal illness and fend off viruses, infections and other diseases.

Surgeons notice when operating that many of their patients show signs of past infections and tumours that their bodies naturally dealt with and got rid of. We're all exposed to viruses and bugs every day, but our immune systems naturally deflect most of them. By thinking positively about our health and its inherently protective mechanisms, we help them continue to work well and do their job of keeping us clear of illness.

All aspects of a positive attitude to life help us live healthily. When we feel positive, calm and content all kinds of physiological functions improve: for instance our blood circulation tends to be good and that helps our hearts to work well. Feeling good, we give our bodies and minds every chance to run smoothly and comfortably. Positive thinking also helps us prevent or quickly and constructively dispel stress, anxiety and depression, which if allowed to get worse or become chronic may have as adverse an effect on our physical health as our mental health.

It also feels good to know that you do have a lot of influence on your general health. Another way to empower yourself, at the same time as giving your natural healing system a helping hand, is to keep up to date with health information. Modern information technology and an excellent selection of well-written books make it easy and interesting to research health issues and being well-informed helps us realize we can take some responsibility for our own health decisions. With our excellent doctors and medical resources as well as trained and experienced complementary medicine practitioners, we can get personal expert advice with second opinions if we wish. So whatever happens to us we can always review the options we have and the benefits of the various treatments. Just realizing this can have a huge effect on our positivity, energize us and give us strength too – all healing effects.

One doctor urged me to write about the importance to our overall health of forgiving ourselves for things we do or have done in the past that could have adversely affected our health. Feeling guilty for being a heavy smoker, for instance, is a kind of negativity that won't help your health now if you no longer smoke and won't necessarily stop you smoking if you still do. Better to wash the slate clean of guilt and regret and look positively at the state of your health today and think how you can look after yourself the best way, lovingly and tenderly caring for yourself. Being kind to ourselves instead of beating ourselves up about what we should or should not have done gives us a lift that is far more likely to enable us to enjoy our health and look after it now.

Personally, this attitude has often helped me not indulge in something – or too much of it – that I realize isn't good for me. For instance if I've thoroughly enjoyed a good meal and am tempted to have seconds, I try to remember to pause momentarily to ask my body how it feels about it. Very often the answer comes instantly back 'That was delicious but I've had plenty thank you!' And I know alcoholics and drug addicts find it a helpful technique when they're in recovery but on the brink of lapsing. By asking themselves if it's what they want, mind, body and soul, or if it's their addiction talking, they show self-respect and recognition of their willpower too and in so doing find it much easier to say no, they don't want it.

I find this approach of respecting and valuing our autonomy regarding our health really inspiring. The concept that health starts today and we can look after ourselves really well – the best we can, the most lovingly we can – being truly good to ourselves, is life-affirming and feels good. Yes!

Accept and enjoy the ageing process

Is this truly possible? Yes it is, very much so. Obviously it's not pleasurable when a part of your body deteriorates as you age; it can be a downright nuisance and at worst, painful. But the progress of the birth–life–death cycle is bound to cause wear and tear, and calm acceptance helps us cope with this, while taking a positive approach to growing older helps us enjoy life anyway and appreciate the benefits, of which, surprising though it may seem, there are plenty! Also – and this makes a huge difference to the whole experience of ageing – it puts us in an excellent frame of mind to pay attention to our health and do what we can to keep everything working as well as possible, minimizing discomfort and continuing to enjoy life to the full whatever our age and condition.

Every stage of life has its complications and compensations. In our younger years we lack experience and probably to some extent self-knowledge and understanding, but we have supple, naturally fit bodies and the natural physical beauty and glow of youth. In the middle years – from around 35 to 55 – we reap the benefits of our maturing minds and growing soulfulness. Physically although we begin to notice signs of ageing like not quite so supple skin, we continue to be fit and full of energy – but there are many demands and pressures on us, so that's just as well. It's as we grow older that signs of ageing creep up on us faster: a few health problems that need tending, maybe, and cosmetic changes as our hair greys and skin sags or gets wrinklier. But this is – if we allow it to be – the richest time of all for self-understanding and cherishing. It's a time for enjoying so many wonderful memories and illuminations, as well as new experiences to warm us and new insights to further develop our minds.

In all the phases of our lives we appreciate the benefits of maturing most if we take a positive attitude to the path of life. None of us knows how long we will be here on this planet, and each day is a gift of a new sunrise and sunset. This is an inspiring way to think of our whole life – we experience the beauty and excitement of birth and live all the constantly changing nuances of shade and brightness through the years as our sun progresses towards the later beauty of its setting, dusk and eventually, the final peace.

Those who believe in a life force beyond the world we know hope for another life for their souls or, as in the Buddhist tradition, that their spirit will be re-absorbed into the universal life. We don't know what will – or indeed, won't – happen and ever since I was a small child I've thought that this is part of the excitement of growing older and that, apart from the wonder of birth, death is the greatest adventure.

If we believe death is the end of us, body, mind and soul, then we can look forward to the perfect peace of it.

Either way, it's positive, so let's not dread death but accept its inevitability with equanimity, determining meanwhile to value each day and enjoy it as much as we possibly can.

I worked with very elderly people for many years and loved their wisdom, spirit and gentleness. It often struck me how individual their approach to life was and the huge effect their positivity – or lack of it – had on their everyday happiness.

Three stand out in my memory as shining with happiness. All had a good sense of humour. Each had their own particular enthusiasm, as well as a general enjoyment of life. One woman in her 90s who liked us to call her by her first name, Margot, adored my cat, Tabitha, who had taken to her, and insisted that she sleep on her bed as often as she wanted to. The little cat kept her company through a long illness and helped keep her spirits high even when the cancer was causing a lot of pain and through her last days. Then there was Mrs Bagshaw, who had had a somewhat lonely life but blossomed in her years with us. She loved to sit in or walk around the garden and to sit at the kitchen table helping prepare vegetables for lunch. I can hear her laugh now – a real delighted chuckle as though she was surprised at her good fortune in her life to become so full of love and happiness at this late stage. And I loved Mrs Castle too, a very down-to-earth multi-millionaire heiress who eschewed airs and graces and liked nothing better than to share a joke with the staff and other carers and friends and invite us to the regular champagne parties she threw, the last one being a celebration of her one hundredth birthday.

All three refused to moan, even when they were too ill or frail to walk and needed nursing round the clock. All three had a positive attitude to life. All three were keenly interested in others, right to the end. All three were demonstratively loving and delighted in being loved and cared for. All three, when their time came, were glad for the life they'd had and died peacefully.

They, and so many other wonderful characters who sailed through their last years, have given me a fantastic example of ageing well. These are the lessons they taught me:

▶ As a general principle, don't be glum, be glad.
▶ Even if physically things become pretty dire, find something to be cheerful about in the present, and delight in happy memories too.
▶ Laugh. Smile. Giggle. It's the most amazing tonic.
▶ Love others whenever you can, try to see some good in them when you can't, and remember you don't know what they're going through.
▶ If you're well enough, do something active.
▶ Sit or walk outside in the fresh air; to feel the sun on your face, or look at flowers and smell them is a little bit of heaven.
▶ Be generous – random acts of kindness, however small, lift your spirits as well as others'.
▶ Don't waste precious life by worrying about ageing and the end of life, accepting instead that they are a natural part of our cycle.
▶ Be glad for every day given to you, and make the very most of it!

Come to think of it, together, they are a recipe for enjoying not just old age, but every stage of life. Positivity, peace and passion – they make us shine whatever our age.

8

Making it happen

In this chapter, you'll embrace positivity when you:
- *Know how you want to live your life*
- *Dream!*
- *Think logically through possibilities and true potential*
- *Make a map of your life*
- *Make plans and focus*
- *Become your own PR officer*
- *Find your own mentors and be one for others*
- *Live in the moment and use it!*

Bringing about the kind of life you deep down hope for and know in your heart is not only right for you but possible, takes a mixture of different ingredients – and the recipe will be entirely your own because you and your life are unique. There are any number of excellent books on 'how to do *xxx*' for every aspect of life you can think of, but they will only be helpful if you, in yourself, are sure of the path you're on or want to follow. Positive energy transforms gut feeling, wishes, ability, hope and ambition into *your* meaning of life, *your* way. And it floods your true path with light so you can see and love the place where you are now and the way ahead. When you follow your own path positively, your confidence and personal power will flow with you, enabling you every day, every step of the way.

> *Each day comes bearing its own gifts. Untie the ribbons!*
>
> Ann Schabacker

Live your life the way you want to

How do you want to live your life?

Pause for a moment.

This is a powerful question – the most important question you'll ever ask yourself. You may already know how and be doing it – if so, that's great! If not, you've a truly wonderful journey ahead as you start to think about and focus on all the aspects. So much has influenced your lifestyle and inner way of being that it can take time to see the direction you'd like to be going in and the place you really want to arrive at. Enjoy mulling it over – it's interesting and satisfying so take your time and enjoy, but try not to procrastinate for ever, as even more fulfilling and enjoyable than thinking about the life you want is living it!

Understanding the purpose of your life means knowing yourself and giving yourself the chance to live at peace with yourself. Instead of stumbling along from day to day, year to year, you'll glide as though on skates. You'll have a feeling of flow and well-being and a great alchemy of intent and satisfaction.

When you hold a picture of the right way forward clearly in your mind, it is in front of you for you to walk into.

It's not about having a startlingly 'successful' life – as far as other people see success, that is. For despite the fascination with celebrities, most of us don't actually want to stand out from the crowd ourselves, or feel superior in any way, and we sense that contentment is most often found in simple and everyday lives and circumstances. And it may have nothing to do with a career as such either. It may be the opposite in fact – that you eschew the conventional work ethic of today and are most fulfilled and content – deeply content – to be at home looking after the family, or in an undemanding job, or perhaps listening to your heart's desire by doing voluntary work. But if you do have the inner knowledge that you have another vocation – for example in the arts, science or entrepreneurism – then that is the path to find and follow.

You may know already what you are here for, or it may take weeks, months, even years to work it out and even then things might change – but the whole journey is interesting and deeply satisfyingly.

It's like coming home and being at home with the self who has always been part of you, of course, but has somehow stayed out of focus much of the time. It's complex as it's as much about your relationship with the world and the environment, and your relationships with your loved ones, as the nature of your inner self. How you find out the way you want to live your life is a very personal thing and you will get there in your own time and style. All I'd suggest is that you're aware of and shut off the voice of your ego. It's easy to recognize it – it's the one that demands 'I want' all the time, usually talking of money and material things.

Here are some questions to get you pondering about what your story is, here on this earth:

- ▶ Who are you?
- ▶ What are you?
- ▶ Why are you here now – at this particular time in the world's story?
- ▶ Where is the right area for you to live, work, play and relax?
- ▶ Why are you here – what are you here to contribute?
- ▶ How can you fulfil your purpose here taking in all the above?

Now take an A4 sheet of paper and write at least 20 words – or as many as you like – in response to each of the above letting the words flow from you on to the paper.

What you see on the paper is an abstract impression of you. It may not be quite you, or the whole you – you've only just started the quest after all but what you've written is very much *about* the real you, the inner, deep, unique being you really are and the meaning and purpose of your life here in this wonderful world.

Dream!

It's so pleasant to dream and it's so good for us too.

In daydreams we can shine as bright as we like and explore all kinds of avenues. When we dream of how we would like our life to be it feels wonderful in the moment and the positivity of dreaming works in other ways too. Many believe that in creating a dream, we somehow give it the chance to become real, as though the light and the vision can't resist spilling over into real life. I don't know how this happens, and of course it by no means always does – as the old adage goes: 'If wishes were horses beggars would ride' but I've experienced it many times myself and I've witnessed it happening to others too.

The concept of luck is very similar. When we consider ourselves lucky and fortunate, good things tend to happen more and more. Another saying goes: 'We make our own luck', and there's always plenty we can do to make things happen and positively adjust our lives in the direction of how we'd like them to be.

When we think of ourselves as lucky, fortunate people we automatically feel good. Putting our positivity into practice, we become better at seeking out openings and following them through, and more effective in everything we do. It's very much about being realistic and practical and working with true, do-able possibility, and at the same time letting our spirit shine too. While being realistic we can recognize our individual personal potential and think sideways as to how we can make the very most of it, our own unique way.

There are several explanations for this phenomenon. Perhaps there is a natural creativity at work which encourages the dream to become a reality. Many believe there is a field of positive energy that we tap into. Or it could be that the positive mind-set somehow attracts serendipitous luck. More prosaically, once we've had the dream, our mind, consciously and subconsciously, has something to work towards and act on, especially if we give it a helping hand by using any of the positive strategies suggested in this chapter and throughout the book. Also, of course, by looking out for opportunities and being ready to take them we increase our prospects.

It's not always the right time for action though, however much we dream and think positive and lucky! We may have natural periods of being in limbo and feeling stuck, when we need to relax and not keep striving fruitlessly to shift things. Sometimes there is no answer right now, or no change possible anyway– for instance at certain times in our lives we may have family commitments that inevitably soak up our time and energy.

Lack of direction may also be a sign we need to lie fallow for a while. I remember one long spell in my career as a freelance writer when work dried up and although I wanted and needed to move to a smaller home, I couldn't find anything suitable. After fretting and hustling as I anxiously tried to make something happen, I decided to draw down the hatches and patiently sit out the storm. I planned a way to bring in enough funds to keep going for the time being while I dreamed about what to do next and waited to see what would come up. I was aware that perhaps I was being guided, albeit against my will, to do something different with my life, change my work in some way or completely. I decided to be totally open about the future.

I've often advised others in similar positions to do the same thing: relax and live in the question, and dream. It doesn't mean you stop watching out for opportunities and openings – it's rather that you stop obsessing about finding or being handed a perfect solution instantly. Now and then through life we all experience storms and lulls, peaks and troughs as well as long periods when all is going well and equably. Whenever I've been in one of the not-so-good-times, I've noticed that as soon as I stop struggling and getting frustrated with what isn't happening to my liking, and accept the wait, my new patient attitude invites in a hugely welcome feeling of serenity and faith that all will, eventually, be well again. As Shakespeare wrote: 'Time and the hour run through the roughest day' (*Macbeth*, Act I Scene III).

I'll keep working at something because that's my nature and meanwhile, always, I keep dreaming. And what happens is that out of the blue things start to happen. Circumstances change of their own volition, or doors open spontaneously or when I gently push them. That time, a project I'd been helping a friend with developed a life of its own and led me into a field I'd dreamed of before but never really thought I'd be able to go into professionally. It was an unexpected delight, born of a dream and serendipity.

This experience helped me counsel a man who was going through the doldrums having been made redundant. He loved his line of work and was keen to continue it, but worried that he was being irresponsible and should take the work he was offered in other fields, just to keep the cash flow going. Fortunately, he was able to rejig his finances to give him a maximum period of a year in which to pick up the threads of the work which at the moment he feels is what he needs to be doing. This is what he told me when he came to see me six months later, to bring me up to date with his news:

'I'd worked so hard to dream my work dream and live it and I knew I had to get back to it, somehow. I needed someone to understand

and reassure me this was valid, hence I came to you. I hated it when well-meaning friends tried to galvanize me into action like pestering companies for work when I knew they had thousands of applicants and I wasn't quite right for them. Or they'd advise me to go and work in the local supermarket or whatever they thought I should do to get some sort of work back on track. In my heart I knew I needed to lie fallow unless and until I ran out of savings and was forced to work at something that wasn't my vocation. I was burnt out and disappointed, and just needed to be able to hold on to my happiness through my everyday life at home.

'It turned out my instinct was right. An opportunity came up that could have been, and I think was, made for me and I was prepared and ready to spring into action. The calm of the long limbo time had somehow replenished my inner energy and gave me the wherewithal to make the move – the post was in Sweden – and get back into the thick of it.'

We may encounter blocks in life when our path is impeded and while accepting change, sometimes it's not right to force it but best to go with the flow, stop beating ourselves up and dream very positively, very lovingly and faithfully, of finding the right way forward again at the right time. When we don't have a destination to travel towards, we need a safe haven to wait in, and dream.

There are also times when even the most fortunate of us experience losses and traumas. However, even when we're grounded by sorrow, illness, hardship or shock, the very act of remembering we still have the ability to think as positively and constructively as possible is a lifeline to hang on to and help us through the bad times (see Chapter 5).

Sometimes we're not blocked by events, but only by our own lack of imagination or self-confidence. So if you happen to feel aimless, apathetic or simply stuck, a good question to ask yourself is 'Do I have any blocks at the moment. Am I impeding the flow of my meaning, my true joy in life?' Just becoming aware of it, if you are, will register as a relief. 'Ah…that's it…now I can do something about it!'

It can be that life is going along reasonably well, with no major problems. Everything should feel hunky-dory. But many people have a persistent feeling there is something more in life for them if only they knew what. They have no burning ambitions or even extravagant wishes. They smile wryly and josh they don't know what they want to be when they grow up. They are cruising along on autopilot, and although their life is partly satisfying, they know they want something that's more truly them. Dreaming is a wonderful way to get ideas and you may be lucky and hit on the one that's just you. But what often happens is that two or three of them will become real possibilities and can be processed and progressed. Living a multi-stranded dream can enable you to find out which is the one you want to flow with and glow with.

Once, as a quite young woman, I shared offices with two other women. We had all left jobs to go it alone, each of us having saved enough for the first year, so we didn't have a lot of time to make things work. Each of us had two or three ideas we knew we'd enjoy building on, but had no idea which would be the one that would do best and that we'd like best. We figured that with more than one string to our bows we'd have a good chance of finding the right dream to follow! It was fascinating how each of us found our niche during that year. Penny soon found she was gravitating constantly towards the personnel consultancy side of her business. It had quickly begun to do well and continued to flourish with her love and care. Jacky soon realized that what she really wanted to do was use her experience in real estate and grow the property management company she'd started in a very small way and which was already beginning to do well. I'd been working in public relations and wasn't sure which aspect to follow through, but soon found that I loved writing best of all. The copywriting turned out to be my path first to journalism, and then, after my psychotherapy and counselling training and many years of experience, to writing self-help and inspirational books and being an agony aunt and advice columnist.

All of us had dreamed of being self-employed but weren't sure exactly how to make it work. By letting the dream run, in several possible ways, we gave it a chance to show us how it wanted to manifest. For each of us, it turned out to be a path we loved and it felt as though it had been there waiting for us to be ready to take it.

Your path will be unique to *you* because you and your abilities, talents and enthusiasms are a very personal mix. But we can all find our path if we have a dream and let it flow in the direction and manner that's right for it and for us. Positivity will help you recognize opportunities and find the openings and directions.

Because daydreaming is discouraged at school, and at home so many things vie for a child's attention, you may not have had the chance to develop the habit of dreaming. Don't worry – you have a great pleasure in store! It's a bit like meditation in that first you empty your mind of everything going on in your life, but instead of keeping it empty of thought, you free yourself to imagine and make up stories or pictures of whatever you wish, with yourself in the middle, having a fascinating time. Dreams can be about anything, absolutely anything. Keep them positive by saying no to any worrying thoughts that happen to pop into your mind, and firmly steer your dream back to goodness and positivity. Remember this is purely for you and your enjoyment, an oasis of calm and pleasure.

In any daydream you may or may not learn something about yourself and your purpose and path in life, and perhaps something creative will come from it, perhaps not. But by daydreaming regularly and often, you invite your subconscious, your creativity and your spirit to speak out and show you insights and possibilities.

Sometimes you feel deeply rested as with meditation, sometimes excited and uplifted. Sometimes you'll find yourself with a partial or even fully formed great idea, or with a new or deepened understanding. It's valuable in all kinds of ways – goodness knows why they don't put it on the curriculum at schools! But now you are in your prime, your mind and time are your own so don't just give yourself permission to dream, but positively encourage it.

The rest of this chapter is all about ways we can take our dreams further when we wish to. That of course requires realism and a practical approach. But however down to earth you have to be – and you will, no question – don't ever stop dreaming. It's so positive and lets your personal power blossom.

Think logically

As you dream and let your positivity flow, ideas will mysteriously start coming to you and two things tend to happen. Some people chase around from one to another, changing their mind and their focus continually and never actually taking any of them forward. Like armchair travelling, this is fine if it's what you enjoy – living in the possibility and living vicariously does suit some of us. But if you want to be active with your possibilities and take a dream forward, you'll want to know that (a) it really is a good one (b) it's worth progressing and (c) it's viable.

These are the basic questions that apply to the smallest possibilities of everyday life right through to the grandest of projects. Even – or rather especially – the most inspired and daring figures, including great entrepreneurs, explorers, and political leaders, need to ask them too.

Many people think a negative attitude is healthy and essential in many areas of life. I agree. Yes, I know, this is a book about positivity and I'm not deviating from that. For when it's sensible to be cautious, a negative attitude is in fact 100 per cent positive!

Optimism is fine as long as it is realistic. If it isn't, pessimism is clearly the sensible, positive route. The key question to ask is 'What will happen if this goes wrong in some way or fails? What will be the consequences?'

As a matter of course, with any new venture or idea, I look at it from all angles and confront the worst scenario that could happen, and the likelihood of it doing so. Sometimes people will say to me: 'Jenny – you're being negative!' But I'm not – it's simply wise to consider all aspects of something new, and however it influences your decisions you will feel good for having faced the dangers. Once you've weighed them carefully, you are in a good, very positive position to decide whether to proceed.

A positive decision combines common sense and intuition. They are independent and co-operative elements. If you find yourself balancing on the brink, either one or both may be warning you the new idea isn't right for you.

A very successful businessman once gave me some advice when I was fretting about my decision not to go ahead with an idea I'd been enthusiastic about. It was helpful at the time and continues to be. He said: 'Some of the best deals are the ones you walk away from.' It applies to all sorts of things including the small choices we may have throughout the day, business opportunities and relationships. Often although there's a lot to be said for one course of action, there's too much against it to take a chance on it. Or perhaps we might have an inexplicable gut feeling that it's not right for us. Either way, withdrawal isn't negative, it's a positive, wise decision and course of action.

Most of the time, we'll never know what would have happened if we had proceeded. Occasionally someone else will take the idea and make it work spectacularly well and you'll find yourself thinking: 'That could have been me – I could have been successful with it!' That's fine. It was their path, not yours. You will have other paths that work for you and are right for you. That's positivity. The energy will intrinsically be there for you if and when the time is right.

Movement through everyday life, whether it's through the familiar routines and tasks or the wider picture of new projects, takes energy and the more positive you are, the easier and more enjoyable it is.

Whether you're considering the plan in general or different aspects of it, it's as important to be both logical and practical about it as it is to let your spirit sing and fly with it. Each approach has its own kind of positive energy, and painstaking thoroughness and inspiration work well together – in a way pacing each other and not letting either get out of hand, and also complementing each other as they help the momentum continue.

It's like running a marathon. All the runners are capable of going the distance, but it's the ones who know how to pace themselves and keep their spirits high who do best and enjoy it most.

Make a map of your life

One of the most rewarding and eye-opening projects I did during a spell at art college was to paint a big map of my life. It was a cross between a diagram, a timeline and a picture that would be aesthetically pleasing too. It was quite a challenge deciding how to do it, but once I got going it was the best fun. It was also, at times, very emotional and it taught me a lot about my life, getting it all into perspective, and helped me see where I was at the time and where I was going, just as the clearest maps do. The theme was the path of my life, which wound in curves and across hill and dale over the canvas. I surrounded it with a frame made up of playing cards, each one illustrating a significant happening in my life, as though we are dealt a hand of cards.

Another way might be to make a big jigsaw puzzle, collage or patchwork quilt, each piece representing an aspect of your life, or to forge a timeline on many levels, illustrated by thoughts and happenings that were and are meaningful to you.

Do have a go at this – it's so illuminating, feels good and gives you a precious, very personal artwork – maybe it will become a family heirloom too.

The main benefit of personal map-making is that you'll realize how full your life has been and how much you've learned. This is satisfying and fulfilling n itself. You'll sense the life energy running through it all and that's inspiring – for the energy, your positive power, is still with you right now and will be there to help you throughout your future too.

Your picture will also be very effective in helping you map out your future – whether it's just for a current project that's important to you or for the whole of your future life.

If you're not sure how to go about it, look at some maps and paintings. Which ones particularly appeal to you? How would you like yours to be? Choose a style that really resonates with you and gives you a thrill. It could be based on pictures or simply text and a diagram if that feels right, or a mixture of both. I used pictures – very naïve stick figures as drawing isn't my metier, but in bright colours they look really good – and also words, and the cards were mostly words but very colourful. A friend made a stunning quilt, every piece meaningful to her in some way.

It somehow gives you great compassion for yourself and the characters who have peopled your life. As various parts of the map reminded me of particular episodes and loved ones I frequently found myself laughing, joyous or tearful – but the latter in a good way.

It's a delight to do, and very positive. And tremendously helpful not just in getting the past in perspective, but in imagining and imaging how you see your project – or life – going ahead.

Make plans and focus

When a dream becomes a very positive idea that you want to progress, the next step is to say to yourself:

'This is a good idea. How can I make it happen?'

Focus and purpose are the foundations of achievement. Positivity is the energy that helps you put the building blocks of your plans together. How well the building goes depends on your attention to detail and your joy in the whole process and your vision of how it will be.

Dreams, wishes, paths, maps, plans – the more detail you put into all these the better. The subconscious loves clarity and will do its utmost to bring about the future that's right for you. Perhaps the universal consciousness works with us too. However the energy that brings dreams into being works, it's very focused and very thorough – so you need to be too, as what you ask for may come into being. There is an old saying, 'Be very careful what you wish for', and it's excellent advice. We need to be sensible; we need to seek only the path that will be good for us not just in the immediate future but in the long term.

Positivity is about goodness, truth and love. As long as we stick to this and don't get carried away with irrelevant and irreverent thoughts of money, material goods and incompatible infatuations, we open the doors for fortune to flow in the direction we hope for.

There we can shine and enjoy deep inner peace and happiness.

Plans, especially, need to be detailed, as they are the blueprint of what you need to do and they help you organize everything in a logical, do-able order. The more time you spend at this stage, the more time you'll save in future and the easier you'll find it to process and progress them.

If you're in business, or want to start one, there are excellent books full of expertise on every aspect. From writing business plans and start-up proposals through cash-flow forecasts, funding, running order and marketing there are comprehensive advice, inspiration, support and strategies to help you.

In life generally, these are my favourite guidelines and on-going sources of inspiration which help me, very positively, with specific ideas and in everyday life.

▶ Every day is a blank page for you to fill, use and enjoy. Every day you can channel your energy as you decide to. The key factor is to be fully involved with your quest to follow your path the best way you can. Every day will be a mixture of finding solutions and developing your plans, always moving forwards compassionately and passionately.

Tip: Imagine you are holding the day in the palm of your hand. What would you like to see in it? How is it formed? Remember, however much detail you incorporate, your day is a living, changing thing so be prepared to be flexible and go with the flow of energy and events.

▶ It's much about balancing. Balancing your time with that of others and your needs with theirs. Be confident you will have ample energy – when you make time for you to do what's right for you, it flows naturally. The momentum, once started, will keep going right through the day in the wave of energy it creates.

Tip: Sometimes pause what you're doing and breathe deeply and slowly. On each in-breath, imagine you are absorbing energy, confidence and enthusiasm; as you breathe out, imagine any negative emotions defusing and leaving you.

▶ Whatever your goals, remember you don't have to reach them all at once. One step – and it can be a small one – starts every mission. One tiny ripple of motion turns into a wave that will carry you along until you decide it's time to stop.

Tip: Rather than letting the whole picture of something you want to do daunt you, think of just one thing you can do now to get or keep it under way. Let 'one step at a time' be your mantra.

▶ Positivity is almost tangible when you make a list of things to be done. Many people recommend having two – one prioritizing what must be done today, the other one that can run on. I prefer to have one, with priorities starred. So often what seems frighteningly daunting is miraculously tamed when the various factors and steps are clearly itemized. It's so satisfying to cross off the things you've done.

> **Tip:** Whenever you don't know where to start, make a list. Then choose one thing from it to do. Choose either something you'll enjoy doing, or the thing you'll be most pleased to have done!

▶ Discuss what you're doing with positive, inspiring people who have the ability to understand your vision, may give you sound advice, and may be constructive about making it happen.

> **Tip:** Think of someone you can phone or meet who will advise or help you in the way you most need at the moment.

▶ Be clear about what needs doing and ready to set boundaries for yourself and others. It's good to know exactly what's what and how far you're willing to go, so you and they will benefit.

> **Tip:** Take time regularly to do a reality check on your time-table and projects.

▶ Be flexible. This may sound like it contradicts the above advice, but knowing nothing is set in stone gives you the freedom to make changes to plans when it's sensible – or even when a wild card comes up that your intuition tells you to play.

> **Tip:** Imagine shaking yourself up so that you get a new, fresh outlook on any over-entrenched ideas, habits and opinions.

▶ Remember it's fine to enlist help. So often we wade through worry and pressure, thinking something's impossible for us, when all the time there's help available. Ah, the relief when we see it or source it – and commission or accept it enthusiastically and gratefully!

> **Tip:** Imagine casting a net wide for help and support and be ready to accept it when you find it.

▶ Punctuate your day with praise for anyone, including yourself, who shows initiative, works well and is nice to be around. Praise makes us glow with pride and the energy released adds extra power to the day's wave.

> **Tip:** Enjoy saying something nice to someone and seeing their pleasure too.

▶ Look for opportunities to feel inspired. Whenever you are, show it, and you're sure to be inspiring too – it's infectious and lights every one up and the atmosphere around you. People and places that are full of inspiration positively crackle with feel-good energy.

> **Tip:** Don't just wait until you feel inspired – look for inspiration, find it and share it with zest.

▶ Avoid running around in circles, fretting, doing too many U-turns or faffing about. Follow your path whether it's straight or gently curving and take time to look at the scenery, relate to others and love them and your work along the way.

> **Tip:** Imagine the path stretching ahead and the pleasure you're going to have and give as you follow it.

▶ Take time to rest and recharge. Even a few minutes of meditation or daydreaming can fire you up to get going again and run smoothly – no pressure, no stress, just the right energy for whatever you're doing and for enjoying the process and the flow.

> **Tip:** Just for a few moments close your eyes (in the solitude of the bathroom if it's difficult to be on your own elsewhere). Breathe slowly. Relax any tensed muscles. Feel stress leaving your mind as well. Register your energy and positivity flowing through you again.

▶ Be re-visionary. If you're flagging, remember your original vision. Live it again and feel the inspiration, excitement and energy of it.

> **Tip:** Shut your eyes and see your vision as a vibrant, colourful picture that you just love, or as a symphony of sound that moves you hugely. Feel it firing up your positivity and renewing your inspiration and resolve.

Become your own PR officer

Positivity is the energy that brings PR – public relations – to life. It also has an important impact on personal relationships as PR is about building a rapport with everyone we're associated with whether at work or at home. In business this may comprise employees, customers, investors, voters and the general public. The term PR often refers to publicity too – always promoting a positive image and constructively dealing with and if possible trouble-shooting anything negative that crops up. As long as PR is honestly positive it benefits everyone.

And so it does when we do our own PR, positively and enthusiastically presenting as honest a picture of ourselves as we can. It's about being open about the good side of your personality and the way you live, and working to be truthful about any struggles with negativity you may have too, for instance the grouchiness we all experience sometimes.

We all have flaws and faults, of course we do. No one is positive, in all senses, all the time. We all have a darker side to contend with and many have to fight hard against depression or behaviour problems.

Personal PR is a great gift in helping us maximize the good about us and minimize the not-so-good. This doesn't mean putting a false face on or hiding behind a less-than-true image in any way. It's about owning up and showing up, being there for people, our true selves and transparent. That way the light – our light – can shine through us and people can relate to us, and we to them, in an honest and very real way.

The great positive effect of doing our own PR is that in the process we notice every bit of ourselves and can see clearly every aspect that we can improve, enlighten, polish up or even clean out completely. PR isn't just about promoting the good bits – it's about de-cluttering, streamlining what's good, and creating a mainly positive wholeness.

As we saw in Chapter 1, a positive attitude is your choice, and this is very much so in regards to your personal PR. If people know you're genuine, they will accept what you tell them and what your attitude, aura and demeanour suggest. So if, for instance, you put yourself down constantly, and come across as someone who can be walked over, they will tend to treat you as though you're incompetent and, whether consciously or unconsciously, they may assume they can walk over you and try to.

The quickest way for someone to stop being a victim is for them to realize that they need no longer think of themselves as a victim but instead recognize they possess inner personal power and are actually surprisingly and effectively strong and able.

So always give yourself a 'good press'. Being prepared not just to speak up for yourself but to behave confidently and self-assuredly not only wins others' respect, but makes you feel really good about yourself. It's positivity in action and very vibrant and powerful.

It's as though a feeling of inner strength creates an aura around us. Not only do we feel strong and psychologically inviolable, but others sense the aura – or perhaps simply see the confident body language, and automatically respect us more.

Many fear self-confidence may lead to arrogance, but with a healthy perspective you'll still keep a sense of humility and beware of straying into the delusion you're somehow better than you are.

As a good meal is food for the body, a good self-image which is also reflected in the image you present to others is food for your psychological well-being. It's wholesome, positive and very rewarding.

Mentors and guides

Through your life you'll have met a few people who've been very special to you on your journey – people who have made you feel especially good about yourself in some way, liking and encouraging you to continue to be your true self, listening to your thoughts and helping you develop them, inspiring you and being inspired by your ideas too. They could be relatives or friends who love you and believe in your ability, or work colleagues who've helped you learn your job and progress in your work. Or they might be people who are accomplished in their own fields and have encouraged you to watch and learn from them.

Value and cherish them or your memories of them, for they are precious diamonds of positivity who can shine in your thoughts all your life through, and who can help you to shine too.

Mentors don't always volunteer themselves. Often we need to find them ourselves.

Looking back at my life so far, I expected to see just a few such people, but to my surprise several immediately step forward in the sunlight of my memory. My parents, a sister, an aunt, two of my parents' best friends, three teachers, two artist friends, two writer friends, two employers, my agent, and a few more dear friends. Also several people who might have no idea how important they have been to me as our contacts were transitory, and yet their impact helped me tremendously along my path.

Goodness – when I come to think of them, how blessed I've been and am and I think you'll be uplifted as you recall your special people too. Take a piece of paper and write down the names of:

▶ Anyone who in raising, teaching and guiding you when you were a child was encouraging, praised you and made you feel you were capable.
▶ Those teachers throughout your life who have sensed the way you best learn and been happy to teach you that way.
▶ Anyone who has helped progress an idea of yours – perhaps just by encouraging you and believing in your ability, perhaps by directly helping you in a practical way.
▶ Anyone you talk to – in person, by phone or by email – who listens to you and does their best to understand you.
▶ Anyone who helps you develop your thoughts and maturity.
▶ Anyone who through their love for you has enhanced your life.

Keep the list somewhere safe for whenever you need reassurance, warmth, love or inspiration.

There will be more mentors and special people in the future. Watch out for them and notice, really notice, the positivity they give to you. Cherish them in the moment as well as in years to come when you look back and see how precious they were to you.

Whenever you have the chance, be a special person to others too. Now you've thought about all the people who have a special place in your heart for the help they've given you, you'll realize how even seemingly small acts of kindness, inspiration and support may be far more valuable than you will ever know.

From a few words of understanding and encouragement to focused, long-term mentoring, you can be an angel.

Your help and inspiration need to be freely given and not in the expectation of reward or reciprocation. But of course you will be richly rewarded anyway, for it's lovely to be kind and thoughtful and it's great, too, to revel in being generous with your time, love and care.

The angel theme reminds me of a story that always makes me smile and I hope will amuse you too. I once took a friend's three young children out for the afternoon and we had a picnic at a popular spot by a stream in the New Forest, as I knew they'd enjoy playing with all the other kids there, which they did. There was a lot of shouting and running about by the stream, and one of the children rushed back to me and said 'Some boys have captured a frog and I'm frightened they're going to kill it.' I rushed over with her and sure enough, this frog was in imminent danger of losing its life. I demanded the thoughtless youngsters give it to me and explained how we should never wilfully hurt any creature. But still unsure if they could be trusted, I and my charges walked a quarter of a mile or so downstream into the quiet of the forest so the frog could go leaping off in safety. Driving home at the end of the afternoon, my car broke down and as we waited for assistance the littlest child, who'd been deep in thought suddenly said, frowning: 'Jenny it's NOT fair. You were that frog's angel. You rescued it and made sure it was safe. God shouldn't have let you break down.'

I had to agree with her, wholeheartedly! But you know even all these years later, I remember the joy of knowing that little frog lived to see another day…

In the film *Amélie* the eponymous heroine does all kinds of things for others without them knowing she's responsible. She delights in their surprise and happiness as much as they do.

Helping others in whatever way we can is one of life's great joys.

Live in the moment and use it!

Time is so mysterious. It can disappear in a flash or drag past. We can cherish it or hate it. We can use it as we wish or let it pass us by.

I beg you to cherish it, use it as positively as you possibly can, be passionate about every precious moment of your life.

Whether you're working, idling, dreaming, planning or doing, be fully conscious. Time enough for oblivion when you sleep. Your waking hours are the chance you have to engage with life, whatever the meaning of your life and wherever your path leads you.

Use your time in the way that's right for you individually. Some of my ideas will work for you but some may not be your thing; so listen to your intuition and self-knowledge. Perhaps, for instance, you're not a list and plan person but are happy and fulfilled meandering as the moment and your mood take you? That's fine. Or perhaps you like to be in detailed charge of every second? That's fine too. Your time – your life – is yours to value and appreciate. You are free and wild and wonderful.

We don't know how long we've got. Hopefully we can look forward to the new expectation of four score years and ten – maybe more, maybe less. I remember my elders warning me that life, however long it may be, disappears faster than we ever think it will and suddenly we're on the last lap. Imagine that! To find yourself on the last lap or the last day, even, looking back and thinking: 'If only I'd done this and this and this…'

How positive and fabulous to look back and know you did most of what you wanted and fully, positively led the life that was yours to live and wasted little of it, and how much easier to accept ageing and, when the time comes, leaving this amazing life and world.

Right now and every day engage with life full on so that your positive power can flow steadily as it's meant to, generating the beautiful kind of energy that lights up life and lets you walk in love and peace and, often, rejoice and dance for joy.

Live in the moment – and love it.

9

Positivity every day!

In this chapter, you'll embrace positivity when you:
- *Cultivate surroundings you enjoy*
- *Look after your appearance*
- *Cherish your social life*
- *Care for your nearest and dearest*
- *Value your work*
- *Enjoy your hobbies and other interests*
- *Troubleshoot difficulties*
- *Recognize beauty and live gracefully*
- *Connect and engage with others*
- *Connect within and beyond.*

Daily life holds us like a cup or bowl, gently supporting our being and protecting us in many ways too. Everyday life, with all its aspects and trappings, shapes how we are and to some extent who we are too. So it's important to adopt a way and pattern that feels good and enriches you. The area or community you live in, your home, how you look and whom you socialize with, your interests and enthusiasms – all these can have a hugely positive daily influence on your well-being.

Some aspects may change little if at all as time goes by, or you may experience all sorts of changes, but by keeping an eye on them all you can check they are still right for you and make any helpful adjustments. Positive thinking will help you choose, influence or adjust your lifestyle in all life's stages and phases to keep that precious quality of life not just comfortable but life-enhancing.

Cultivate surroundings and spaces you enjoy

Being happy with the space around us, even if it's just in some small way, makes a surprisingly big impact on our well-being. Surroundings are important to us and to our positivity and it's so easy to make them more attractive and comfortable.

At work we may not have much choice about the area around us, but we do have influence over it. We can often personalize it and make it look bright and welcoming with a few flowers, for example, or a photo of a loved one. You may like to keep it tidy and smart or, like me, rather like the familiar feeling of an untidy desk and piles of beloved books as long as you have some lovely things and colours around too. We're all different. We all make our mark our own way but often don't stop to appreciate it. Do! Take in the things you like and, if there aren't any, make some. Sometimes we need to think sideways. For instance, employers who insist on no personal stuff around may be very amenable to suggestions for enhancing the look of the whole place.

It makes such a difference to the atmosphere of a place if it's cared for. And art is accessible and affordable now and can uplift everyone's spirits, so again, sensible employers will look favourably on investing in some inspiring paintings or even sculptures.

At home the space really is our private castle. The smallest studio can be comfortable, pleasing on the eye and so a great base and an inspiration for everything you do. You can spend as much or as little as you wish and nowadays, with great community organizations that recycle unwanted goods free of charge, you don't even have to spend anything if the budget is tight.

The secret is to choose things that you enjoy looking at and furniture that's comfortable and practical too. Colour colours our lives and lights up our minds, so opt for shades you love and which complement each other. Don't feel you have to be fashionable – fine if you want, but fine too if you're not in step with whatever's on trend. Trends have a habit of turning full circle so you could be one of the avant-garde!

Aim for a look and feel that gives you a welcoming gladness the minute you open the door and go in and that, when you leave, you look forward to returning to. Such a simple element of life, but when you pause to appreciate it, you'll be bowled over by the way it impacts so positively and even joyously on your well-being.

As well as the visual uplift, and the practical pleasure of living somewhere that makes you comfortable, there's another innate aspect that makes you feel good – expression. Apart from the pleasure of choosing, for instance, colours you love, you'll enjoy the feeling that through them you're expressing your personality and giving an element or the essence of who you are.

This is why it's vital to have colours and things you really love around you. So many people follow fashion slavishly, or entrust the interior design of their home to someone else without making and insisting on a high degree of input. To be sure of loving your habitat, be sure that it speaks to you and of you. Then, for you, it will glow with pleasure and positivity, and so will you. There is a very wonderful energy in a home that's much beloved.

Another way of making your mark

Self expression – for example, engraving your signature, creating a time capsule or improving your home in a permanent way– makes a personal statement that we have been in a place and has an intrinsic feel-good factor.

It gives a feeling of continuity and your presence at a moment in time, however transitory. If you live somewhere that you love in some way, leave something of yourself there – something positive, something good. It could be a permanent improvement you're proud of that other people who live there will enjoy through future years. Or you could make a simple reminder just for yourself that probably only you will know is there, like your signature in an out-of-the-way place. But who knows? Someone might see it in years to come and wonder who you were and wing a word of love and connection to you across the dimensions! This is a centuries-old practice – I so enjoy seeing names etched in ancient churches or antique furniture. The presence of those people is palpable.

Another intriguing idea is to make a time capsule. In a non-perishable little container place some words – a description of yourself, maybe, or something you love like a poem and a good wish for whoever should chance to read it, along with a picture if you like. As you position it, buried deep in the garden, or in a wall that's being replastered, for instance, feel the pleasure of this expression of you that will stay on into the future.

These are such easy, small gestures, but so meaningful and satisfying to do, and in registering your presence now, you will give a similar thrill to others – a moment of connection – perhaps far into the future, long after you've gone.

A sense of place, a sense of you – they link and dance with positive energy and joy.

Look after your appearance

Haven't we remarkably complex bodies and faces? And, though we are alike in so many ways, how different we are from one another too. Our bodies can be such a rich source of appreciation and gladness for us. We don't always notice that there is beauty in every one of us in all phases of life, as artists down the centuries have realized and shown in their work. So perhaps we should see ourselves through the eyes of a master artist and fall in love with every feature of our faces and our astonishingly well-crafted bodies.

It feels good to care for yourself. An essential for an everyday physical feeling of positivity is to keep our skin, surprisingly the body's largest organ, well moisturized and supple and every part of ourselves as fit as possible by eating, exercising and resting well, as described in Chapter 7.

A simple thing to do that feels good emotionally and physically is to lay our hands on ourselves, on different parts, and rest them there, registering how the skin, flesh and bone beneath feel to our palms, and how the touch feels to them. It's such an easy thing to do, but I don't think many of us do it. So try it out. Even somewhere public you can, for instance, lay one hand over the other, or spoon them, and feel the contact and the sense of recognition and love you feel for your so precious hands and for yourself. Perhaps not in public, but when you're on your own, try stroking yourself too, just like you would a cat. Feel how soothing it is and how good and how it makes you feel like purring! The sensation resonates with gentle pleasure – not sexual or even particularly sensual – just life-affirming and positive and I believe it to be very healing.

It's great for self-esteem and self-contentment to look after our personal appearance too – and it gives pleasure to others as well, a double bonus. Again you don't necessarily need heaps or even any make-up – clean hair, well-conditioned skin, sparkling eyes and a bright smile are the simplest of things and they mean you shine with natural good looks. Knowing we look our best lifts our positive energy and puts a bounce in our step.

And to dress attractively and in character is doubly pleasing too. Interestingly, we don't need to spend a lot on clothes unless we wish to. The wealthiest people I've known wore the oldest clothes I've ever seen and were the least concerned with fashion, but they were charismatically attractive. I mention this to point out that a good appearance isn't anything to do with spending a lot. Such people have some key habits which have a hugely positive effect on their appearance, and which are open to all of us to adopt. They are:

- ✓ Walk tall.
- ✓ Move gracefully.
- ✓ Be very, very kind.
- ✓ Enjoy an incredibly infectious sense of humour.
- ✓ Wear your clothes with élan – your way.

Cherish your social life

Friends light up our lives, as they are beacons of camaraderie, support, shared fun and conversation. They affirm that we're likeable and that we enjoy liking others too. Friendship feels wholesome and good. Once again, we're all different in the number and kind of friendships we have. Some people collect loads of friends, some have a few, some one or two. It very much depends on your personality and lifestyle.

Like every other living thing, friendship takes care and maintenance. Our social lives are sure to vary through the phases of life, and the amount of contact we have with friends can vary hugely. But insufficient attention is dangerous because although friendships sometimes survive it, all too often they fade away and either you lose touch completely, or when you try to revive the relationship you've found you've both changed and the rapport you shared is no longer renewable. So even in those times when a friendship is largely in abeyance, think of the person lovingly and take time to make contact at least every now and then with positive assurance of your regard and care for them.

Keeping in touch with our friends isn't hard to do – it's a habit that becomes second nature after a while and is enjoyable in itself. Even an annual 'catch-up' letter, phone call, lunch, email or birthday, Christmas or anytime card will keep the embers of friendship alight. It doesn't take long but the thought behind it means such a lot to the recipient.

Occasionally, when we're not on the same wavelength any more, we may need to face the fact that it's best to let go. Even with a strong friendship, differing interests or likes and dislikes in a new stage of life may reduce your compatibility. It can be difficult, like any loss, and it represents change too. But accepting it gracefully and being ready to move on is a positive way forward and enables you to remember the good times and affection you shared.

Usually though, it's well worth sticking with friendships even when the style or content of the contact you have has changed. Old friends are very, very precious. You know each other so well and you basically like each other. As long as you respect each other's views, accept your idiosyncrasies and are ready to be mutually supportive – and of course can still laugh together – the friendship can sail on enhancing both your lives however much or little communication you have.

It's worthwhile revisiting any lapsed friendships too, unless you know in your heart they are truly over. Websites dedicated to helping people resume friendships, and search engines that make it possible to find old friends, can enable you to get back in touch and then it only takes an email or two more to quickly explore if you still get on and would like to be friends again.

Don't waste energy and emotion on people who don't want your friendship or don't reciprocate it – save it for those who welcome you in their lives and love you. Accept the situation and harbour no hurt or bitterness. Except in extreme cases, don't lock your heart against people you like, even though they've rebuffed your love or offer of friendship. Perhaps one day you will both be at a stage in life where you are on the same wavelength and can then take the opportunity to enjoy the gift of mutual pleasure in each other's company.

The web is also an amazing way to keep connected and to communicate and some friendships exist happily in that medium alone. I write far more letters now, as emails, than I ever did either in handwriting or type as snail mail ones. But do keep in touch by phone and in person too, where possible, as nothing beats hearing a friend's voice for real, and even better being able to give them a hug.

A nice way to remind us to appreciate our friends is to write down their names and for each one, note down your thoughts about them:

▶ Why do they matter to you?
▶ Why do you have an extra soft spot for them?
▶ How do you show it?
▶ How do they make you feel good and inspire you?
▶ What particularly funny or moving moments have you shared?

And now turn the tables and note your thoughts about how good a friend you are to each one:

▶ Why do they love you?
▶ How could you be a better friend?
▶ Whether you are non-judgemental?
▶ Do you help them in some way to feel good about themselves?
▶ Do they inspire you?
▶ Do you make an effort to get on the same wavelength?
▶ Do you think of them lovingly, warts and all?

Friendships are vibrant, colourful parts of the tapestry of life and the contact we make with other people. The experiences we share are the golden threads we weave throughout the years and make a wonderful pattern of positivity and love. It's easy to forget the special moments, though, so try writing yours down. I love to look back through my journal and see the things that made us laugh, cry or puzzle over. I wish my parents and the friends who've passed away had written down their memories. You could write them in your journal or an even better idea would be to have a friendship book so that when you meet they can look through it and you can enjoy the memories together.

Friendship is valuable and worth caring about. Good maintenance enables the rapport between you to shine and whether that's the soft glow of occasional, low key contact or full-on current and active togetherness, it hums with positive energy and love.

Caring for your nearest and dearest

For many of us the love we have for our closest family and friends is the most important thing in life. We show our love in myriad ways and in so many ways, too, it lights up our lives. How vital it is not just to be vaguely aware that we love them and are loved by them, but to actively appreciate it every day and pay attention to our loved ones, lovingly.

Expressing love on an everyday basis is an all-round good. You feel good when you make a loving gesture, they do too, and the atmosphere between you and around each of you is uplifted.

It's about countless things you do for each other – however small, each is valuable, as is appreciation for them.

Words are one of the most obvious ways and it's not just dedicated love words, it's the way we speak to each other too at all times and our body language as we talk and move around each other.

How easy it is, though, to get into a habit of putting each other down. Even when it's allegedly teasing, we need to be careful of our tone and be absolutely sure the one we're mocking, however gently, really does enjoy it. When they do, and the joshing is truly affectionate, it's fine, but beware of hurting them, or by too frequent or over-boisterous bantering making them grow a thick skin of indifference or, worse, emotional scar tissue.

On the whole, be kind, encourage their self-confidence, show them openly you love them without feeling you have to hide it in jokes. And expect them to treat you lovingly too. Every time I hear or see people – whether friends at home or strangers in a supermarket – being caustic to their companions, my heart sinks. I feel like shaking them into recognition of what they're doing and the risk they're taking. Risk? Very much so – there is a great risk that on-going nagging, direct criticism or just looks of hostility or scorn, will sour the relationship and in time seriously damage and even wither the love they share.

It's a safe bet that if you asked, for instance: 'Why did you tell them they're 'stupid'? Don't you love them?' they would protest that they didn't really mean they're stupid, and that of course they love them really. And probably they do. But it's no way of showing it or caring for that love.

Do ensure, with every micro-speck of your body and soul, that you don't in this way sabotage the love you and your loved ones share. What a waste of your time together, for one thing, and how you would regret your behaviour if you found yourself on your own without them. How much better to use your time together positively – it feels so much better for yourself, them and everyone around you.

In everyday life just as much as in those special moments when you happen to feel romantic, it feels so fantastic to be openly loving and loved. Love, expressed, energizes and enhances your whole life even when you're apart.

It's the same with being grudging: crossly doing the shopping or chores round the house, bitterly thinking of how your life could be if you had a different spouse or your kids were better behaved or more successful in some way – what a huge waste of opportunity! They'll sense you denigrating them like this and shrivel a bit inside – and so will you, for bitterness is like bleakly attacking yourself from the inside. Instead, encourage them to be the best they can by showing you have faith in them and being generous with your time, support and love generally and they'll automatically respond by maturing into nicer, more loving people.

Most of the time it's simply a question of choosing that first key to positivity – a positive attitude. Then you'll automatically and even instantly be in the right mindset to take time to listen to them and talk with them, so that you understand each other better. And you'll find you rekindle your interest in them – and theirs in you as you positively choose to take an interest in them – their thoughts, their activities, their emotions.

There is a deep, positive core of respect at the heart of loving relationships. Insist on their respect, respect yourself, and respect them and you will all benefit.

Be open to them, letting them know who you are. And take an on-going interest in them too. Talk about and respect each other's values. Listen to each other's childhood stories, their dreams, ambitions, sorrows, longings, even if you've heard it before. Above all, remember love – what you love about each other and what you can learn to love.

Of course we all – or at least most of us – fall out sometimes. Of course, too, occasionally we annoy or irritate each other. We're human! But just think – imagine it, feel it – what it would be like if they died? Feel the aching gap left, the huge sorrow. It gives a gut-wrenching shock to do this but it's worth it as it will seriously bring home to you how dear they are to you. Think of your love for them and the place they hold in your heart every single day. Be ready to make up quickly, say sorry, accept their apology too and, where necessary, constructively sort out any issues.

Love is the most precious thing you have, the most precious thing in the whole world. Cherish it wholeheartedly. Cherish your dear ones. Love is the most important part of your personal power. Use it with tender care, lovingly and very, very positively.

Working gladly

Isn't it good when someone speaks well of their work? Contrast the feeling this gives you with the one you get when someone else has a negative take on it, in some way denigrating it – 'it's not interesting' or 'it's not what I really want to do', or being self-deprecating: 'I'm hopeless really.'

But when they speak enthusiastically of whatever it is they do, whether it's a career, running a home, being a mum, doing voluntary work, progressing ideas at home, etc. etc. it gives you, the listener, a lift. As you pick up on their positivity their energy flows through you and you feel glad for them and, maybe, inspired to enjoy your work more too or feel empathy with them if you already do.

It's good to work, it's good not to work too. Some of each is ideal as each is balanced and enhanced by the other. When you've done some work, your leisure time feels like a lovely reward and you can relax into it with a happy sigh of self-contentment. When you're relaxed, maybe following a pleasant weekend off, your batteries are recharged and you're ready to get back into work mode again enthusiastically and give it your best.

So let's all be the kind of people who readily own up to being glad we work and enjoy what we do. Some think it's good to be humble and put themselves and their work down because they think it will please others. But in not shining, we spread negative feeling; others might then feel they need to dampen or hide from us their own enthusiasm. Shining with gladness that we do our work and value it, on the other hand, and taking a warm interest in what *they* do, shares your positivity with them, and that's a great gift.

In complete contrast to negativity, there's something wondrously charismatic about this kind of enthusiasm in its effect on others. It gives them permission to openly enjoy the things they do, however simple and everyday. They'll also naturally warm to you for leading with your example of gladness and enabling them to show their own.

The inspiration we give each other isn't just in the moment, either – it can last a lifetime. I remember vividly people from all walks of life who have shone for me. Their example of enthusiasm rings out to encourage me to love my work and be glad to show it and, in doing so, share the positivity. Who do you know who shines like this and makes you smile with their enthusiasm, however quiet or loud, for their work?

Here are some of mine to show the diversity of their paths:

▶ Gwen, who was a needlewoman and tailor. She spent her life sewing and gently shone in the satisfaction of good work.
▶ Joan, who nursed all her life and took pride in ensuring all her patients felt loved and cared for. A true healer. Great sense of humour too!
▶ Andrew, who does all kinds of freelance work and whose great enthusisam energizes everyone he comes into contact with.
▶ Chris and Geoff, both lawyers, whose pride in their work and determination to be scrupulously fair and informed has helped so many.
▶ Mary, now retired as a teacher but always busy nevertheless. In her career as a teacher she shone with enthusiasm and now she works tirelessly caring for others.
▶ Mike, a self-employed builder who delights in doing a good job and having satisfied customers – and as a bonus he's really funny and makes everyone laugh even when their home is temporarily disrupted by the work.

I could go on and on – I've been so blessed with people whose positive work aura has warmed me and helped light up my own gladness in work.

Now make your list and feel the glow of pleasure your examples give you. Then think about yourself and your own work. How does what you say about it and your general attitude to work affect others? If you already show a gladness about work, that's great. Keep enjoying your work and reflecting your enthusiasm in your own way. If you're usually downbeat about it, try turning this attitude around by reviewing all the positive aspects and setting out to actively enjoy them.

It isn't only about the actual work – sometimes not necessarily at all. With any work, even a career you'd rather not be in permanently or those various daily chores that are a must rather than a choice, consciously feel the pleasure of working as well as you can, and the huge satisfaction afterwards. Every day do something that gives you this satisfaction and watch the upward curve of your positivity.

Just think how it uplifts you when your employer and colleagues or anyone around you love their work, or when friends and family do things willingly and cheerfully? Or when people who serve you in shops, catering places and offices are obviously happy with their work and warmly engage with you? The positivity reflects on you so you shine a bit more too. You can have this same effect on others too, every single day. Such positive power, in such an easy, feel-good way, to brighten everyone's day including your own.

Relish your hobbies and other interests

We are blessed with freedom to follow whatever interests we choose in life. And there are so many opportunities and possibilities it's like a smorgasbord of good things spread out for each of us. Bored? How can anyone be bored? Life is a magic carpet of potential offering fascination and absorption in any or all of the options you choose.

Maybe, if your usual interests don't compel and delight you at the moment, it's because you know in your heart they're not the right ones for you? If so, don't waste any more time on them – go forth and search for things that really grab you and are so *you* that you can't believe how they've eluded you before.

Or maybe if you used to love them, you overdid it or became too caught up in competition and that took the edge off your enthusiasm or jaded it? In that case, take a break for a while or step back a little to give yourself a space where your passion can replenish itself and return full-on again. Remember that positivity is something we can choose and guide and that when given this chance to breathe it flows naturally and joyously again, at its own pace.

But if you don't have any hobbies and interests that sing to you, and you with them, then you have delights in store as you explore the options and bring some into being.

We looked at the issue of time in Chapter 3 but as the temptation to say 'But I haven't time,' is so persuasive, let's just revisit it in case it pops up again as you think about your interests.

You do have time. Your life is yours to organize as you wish. Yes, there'll be various commitments and duties, but if you put your mind and positive energy to it you can make time, each day or at least one or two days a week, for your own interests and personal passions.

It's so easy to fritter time away on things we don't want to do and don't actually have to do or need to do. If unchecked, I'd waste endless time when I'm not working on things like flicking through catalogues, surfing the net for no reason and doing Sudoku puzzles. Lots of people play computer games or watch television programmes that they don't positively like or get much from. Then there is text messaging, which can eat up so many precious minutes adding up to hours – but more on this in the next section. Have an honest think whether there are any ways you squander your time and if so make a conscious, very positive decision to cut them down drastically. Encourage yourself by the vision of the time you'll free up.

It can be quite scary to do this, I know. It's much easier to while away time with trivial things that take no effort. Without a doubt, discovering interests and building your rapport with them does take energy, both emotionally and physically, but it's taking the first step that's the most difficult bit. Once you've got over that initial resistance, you'll be away. It's a bit like skating. It's a bother putting the boots on and finding good places to skate – but once you do and you have, you glide along, smoothly and enjoyably making progress.

Interests light up our lives, right the way across the stages and decades. They may stay with you for always or perhaps shift slightly or completely metamorphose into others. But the richness and fulfilment they give you will always stay with you.

Tara was talking of skiing: 'I haven't been for 15 years,' she said, 'and doubt I ever will again. But I'm so glad I did it – I often daydream about it, imagining how it felt, almost being on those skis again, the sound and feel of the snow under them, the pine scent of the forest we sometimes went through and above all the fun. Sometimes it was frightening too – especially getting off those wretched bar-lifts and chairs – but it made us laugh even more! Just think – if I hadn't gone, that first time, I'd have missed all of that. It was such a great experience.'

Strangely enough, it doesn't have to be something relatively exciting to make a lasting impact. I've tried all kinds of things in my life, some exciting, some apparently deadly dull. I remember now, for instance, with a big smile on my face, learning to knit. It wasn't my forte, and that's an understatement! By the time a friend had unpicked and re-knitted for me my third sweater and my husband dolefully said he couldn't wear the socks I'd so lovingly made him, I'd been on a knitting journey that still makes me chuckle today. And when I watched a friend clicking away as we talked the other day, I could feel the needles and wool in my fingers, and the thrill of trying to develop the skill. Even though it wasn't for me, I enjoyed the challenge and overall it was a really good experience!

All your interests, past, present and future, are part of your life's tapestry. Make it rich and beautiful, and not only will you find fun and fulfilment now, you'll create memories to renew the satisfaction in years to come.

They are a part of you, a part of your life: a pleasure and source of so many positive things – happiness, satisfaction, challenge perhaps, fascination and perhaps new skills – all combining in a warm sense of fulfilment.

So many treasures to mine, so many ways to enrich your life.

Troubleshoot difficulties

I love Maya Angelou's observation that you can tell a lot about a person by the way he or she handles these three things: a rainy day, lost luggage, and tangled Christmas tree lights. We can learn a lot about ourselves, too, if we reflect on how we handle them! I usually take bad weather, literally and metaphorically, in my stride, and when an airline lost my luggage it didn't faze me and I enjoyed creating a rapport with the sympathetic and helpful people in customer services as they did their best to locate it and reunite me with it – but tree lights!!! I've learned that it's best to ask everyone else, including cats and dogs, to leave the room so that I can quietly get on with the job of disentangling them without the fear that someone is going to step on them or, in the case of dog and cat, make the tangle even worse!

How do you cope with these situations and other difficult ones? And how do you cope when you're with someone who doesn't cope well at all in any disappointment or difficult situation?

As ever, positivity saves the day if you:

- ✓ Pause.
- ✓ Decide to take as positive an attitude as possible.
- ✓ Think if there's something constructive you can do to ease the situation or solve the difficulty.
- ✓ Breathe deeply and slowly.
- ✓ Consciously relax any tense muscles.
- ✓ Centre your confidence on your solar plexus.
- ✓ Stand straight.
- ✓ Switch your positive power on fully.
- ✓ Remain mindful of others.

I also find it helps hugely to recall my sense of humour if it's gone AWOL, and to reflect whether in the great scheme of things the situation is actually that dire or that important.

On the rare occasions it is, all the above apply and it's even more important to summon all your personal power and common sense and to get support and help from others too. Keep calm, trust your common sense and ability and stay alert but calm and focused. That way you'll stay in touch with all aspects of the situation as best you can and keep it in perspective.

Recognize beauty and live gracefully

Beauty is all around you to see or to sense in other ways. When you have the habit of noticing and enjoying it in even the seemingly smallest of things or the often unnoticed, it instantly gives you a wonderful feeling of positivity and the thrill of joy.

Physically, for instance, you might delight in the classically enchanting scent of a rose, a modern perfume you love or the scent of rain on dry grass; the feel or touch of someone you love; the sound of warm-hearted laughter, music that delights your soul, birdsong; something – anything – that is beautiful to your eyes. It could also be the taste of something delicious and, last but not least, a sense of physical comfort in some way. Metaphysically, the sense of connection with or through other dimensions can be beautiful, and so can our intuition of beauty – in someone's soul, for instance.

Thomas Aquinas defined beauty as: 'that which pleases when seen' but the truth is more: 'that which pleases when sensed' for there are many forms of beauty besides the visual. And any sense of beauty you consciously notice and enjoy will lift your spirits and, if you're willing, quietly or joyously suffuse you with pleasure.

So often people think only of obviously or outstandingly attractive or fashionable things as beautiful. But beware of jading your palate of beauty by looking always for the most extreme. I was interested to read in a food writer's column that he discovered that a very simple, everyday dish he at first thought bland was actually subtly and deliciously flavoured. Watch the food programmes on television and you'll see that mostly the chefs talk of more and more seasoning and spices. Yet the columnist realized that simple foods – bread and cheese, for instance, scrambled eggs or a plain baked potato – are, literally, sensationally scrumptious if you take the right approach. Your sense of beauty can be encouraged and honed when you notice beauty in the myriad small and simple things too.

All it takes to light up your life with beautiful experiences is to use your eyes and all your senses. The world is a living miracle and it's full of billions and billions of miracles of beauty. You'll know them because they make you glow with positivity – and the more you notice them, the more the energy of positivity will flow through you and your life.

Connect and engage with others

When we switch on to daily life and everything that's going on, we automatically connect with the positive energy that's around us and flowing through us all the time. It's about feeling alert and aware, ready to notice things we might otherwise pass by, unseeing and unfeeling.

When you engage fully with what's going on, you pick up on the energy and feel full of life, primed to sense how others are feeling, and how you yourself are.

Positively guard against cruising through the day on automatic pilot. Routine, habit, stress and pressure can all too easily sap or divert our interest and energy from things that really matter or which are full of interest if only we notice them.

Modern technology gives us so much and makes communication ultra-easy. Used well it's a blessing and a joy. But it's also responsible, when misused, for a growing habit of disconnection with the immediate world around us. And it can be a menace when we let it run our lives too. So use it carefully to enhance your life and your connection with friends, at the same time harnessing your positive power to refuse to let it control you and soak up your time unnecessarily.

As mentioned above, I'm thinking particularly of text messaging. Yes, texts are a wonderful way of communicating, but the danger is that they can become an addiction that stops you connecting with the people you're actually with. Think how annoying it is when you're with someone who you really want to talk to and they're repeatedly breaking off to receive or send a text. It's just the same for those you're with when you do it. So resist the compulsion to be constantly available to callers and text messagers.

Notice how positive it feels when you give your full, undivided attention to the person or people you're with. Be brave – switch your phone off so that you can engage positively like this and be fully in the moment with them. Face-to-face contact and talk has a special energy of its own and feels good. Full attention is a lovely compliment to give and receive – in fact it's one of the most valuable gifts there is.

It isn't only phones that distract. Televisions, radios, and even music which is left on when someone visits or telephones damage the interaction between you and can even disrupt it completely. Switch them off. It's polite, it's positive and it's obvious that it's the only thing to do. Again, it pays the compliment of your attention to the visitor or caller. Don't just turn down the volume, as a radio or music speaker playing however quietly, and silent pictures on a television screen, can still steal your attention from the person you're talking with as well as your thoughts from your mind. Switch them right off.

A friend gave me a great tip for dealing with the situation when someone calls just as you're watching or listening to a programme that's important to you: set up a DVD recorder so all you have to do is press a button to record the programme. Then you can fully engage with it and enjoy it once later, when you can give it your undivided attention, which is freed up meanwhile for the person you're talking to.

I used to think that I could multi-task, taking a telephone call as I did some research on the internet, or even continuing to write. But I learned that it's not possible to fully engage with the person you're on the phone to. Now I either press the button that turns the screen display off, or get up and walk away from the computer so I can give them my full attention. Again, it's a compliment and a courtesy as it allows a full connection and that feels good and is very positive.

These may seem pernickety small things, yet paying attention to them enables you to pay attention to those you're talking to, and that's one of the most important things in any interaction. Funnily enough it's often those who mean most to us whom we pay the least attention to, so watch out for any sign of disconnection. Positive attention is absolutely vital between people who want to establish or maintain a meaningful connection and relationship with mutual understanding. It's at the very heart of love.

Similarly, mindfulness enables us to be aware of all that's going on within and around us in the various activities we engage in throughout the day. Mindfulness is a good word for full attention across the spectrum, as it applies to our body and soul as well as mind.

Mindfulness in the moment means you're present, paying attention, experiencing with all your senses, antennae alert on every front. It enables, even in the most humble or frequently repeated things, a deeper understanding and adds a welcome appreciation of purpose and, surprisingly often, an awareness of enjoyment.

Connect within and beyond

Listen, listen, listen, to your intelligence, within and without. Explore your mind and keep all your antennae alert so that your spirit can soar and fly and come safely home. Always stay in touch – or as close as you can be – with the greater consciousness, the mystery of the energy of this universe and beyond.

Doing this makes our consciousness of being alive meaningful and reminds us how precious life is, every moment.

It can help to remember the atlas or timeline you made of your life and check out where you are on it, this moment, this day. Ask yourself gently how you are – not just physically but mentally, emotionally and spiritually. Feel whether your positive power is flowing, and if you realize it's a bit sluggish or even missing, ask yourself how you can connect with it fully again and help it flow smoothly.

You might like to write something: some notes in your journal, a letter or a poem? Or you could paint a picture of where you are now, as abstract, impressionist or descriptive as you wish.

Or simply be present and feel the positivity of where you are, here, today. Yes, like all of us, you are vulnerable, but be confident of your inner strength too – now, this moment.

Take your search for meaning seriously, at the same time loving the sense of your spirituality. It sparkles like the stars that are made of diamonds but it's more precious – infinitely more precious – than any amount of gems or wealth.

Feel the love that flows through our world and reach for the numinosity of its source. Whether atheist, agnostic or believer we can all feel the magic of that love and the power. And we can all sense the ineffableness of infinity and yet the possibility of parallel universes, untapped energies, other dimensions. We can sense the wonder of it all, each day, value our knowing and at the same time feel the awe and reach out, reach out in love and joy to that connection.

Just for a moment, at least once every day:

- ▶ Pause.
- ▶ Feel – with all your senses, all your antennae.
- ▶ Appreciate your wholeness.
- ▶ Know the wholeness of the greater consciousness.
- ▶ Tingle with the connection.
- ▶ Give thanks and be glad.

Living positively, every day, in all aspects of our being, we open ourselves to the joy of the world, the benevolence of life, and the joy and love in our lives too. Positive energy courses through us and from us and enables us to keep negativity and the sorrows and traumas of life in perspective and, like the world around us, constantly renew, recover and heal.

You are on the path of deep consciousness with a strong, courageous determination to be your true self and live positively. You are prepared not just to join the quest to help our planet's survival but to make life here and now a better place to be for you, your loved ones, others beyond and all animals.

Live a rich life. Be true and honest, brave, thoughtful and prepared to speak your mind. Speak out for goodness, kindness and justice, and delight in the energy of your positivity. Every day, feel it: your presence; the silent hum of energy. Every day make your peace with the world and feel its vitality– raw, powerful, beautiful and positive.

You are part of it!

10

The peace of integrity and truth

In this chapter, you'll embrace positivity when you:
- *Live truthfully and honestly*
- *Have values and integrity*
- *Deal compassionately with hostility*
- *Live as ethically and morally as possible*
- *Live humanely*
- *Live courageously*
- *Live in grace and peace.*

How right it feels and how good and peaceful it is to recognize our innate sense of truth, justice and morality and to abide by it. But how much courage it takes and how tempting it is to step aside! We need every bit of our personal power to help us. Thankfully, it is *always* there for us. Whatever happens to you throughout life and wherever your path leads, a positive attitude together with your reasoning ability will enable you to cope honourably and rightly. Therein lies confidence and a great sense of calm in any circumstances.

Live truthfully and honestly

Like most of us you were probably encouraged to be truthful as you grew up. As kids, we soon learn not to fib as we find we're praised for being truthful and get into trouble if we're not. Later we think it through and make our own decisions, usually settling for truth, at least most of the time, for more reasons than pleasing parents. There are many practical positives – for instance if you always tell the truth you don't have to remember what you've said because the truth is always the truth! Also, others sense honesty and respond well to you, and your loved ones know they can trust you and do. All these practical aspects of being honest keep the wheels of life turning smoothly and mean we enjoy the peaceful path of being trusting and trustworthy.

Another kind of truth that's incredibly important in a different way is your inner sense of truth. We talked about being yourself and knowing yourself in Chapter 2 and I'd like to take this further now and sing praises for the wonderful feeling you will experience on an on-going basis when you live truthfully according to your own reality. That is, you know who you are and are prepared to think your inner truth, speak it, feel it and love it.

Truth is an integral part of our positive power. It shines with passion and at the same time simplicity. It walks with us along the path that's right for us. It shows us the way, always. It protects us from doubt and despair. Truth is a vital part of life. It's only we humans who turn our backs on it – other animals are automatically true to themselves, and the natural world can be nothing else but truthful. One of the fantastic things about this earth is its honesty, almost blinding in its clarity. It simply is.

We are different from other animals, at least so it's assumed, in that we have a special consciousness and a conscience. We are free to see the truth, or choose another way. A philosopher friend said to me: 'Don't tell them it's easy. It's not.' He meant that there are myriad ethical dilemmas and hugely complicated philosophical theories about truth. Yes, he's right. But I think we can make things hard when they need not be. If we listen to our inner being, and follow what we know, deep down, to be the truth, then step by step we will find the way of honesty – the right thing to do in the circumstances. It may not be an easy way, but usually it is. Being human, we may stray, but we can come back to it with more resolve. We know, deep in our psyche, heart, mind and soul that it gives us peace.

Living in truth is not about being dogmatic, affectedly sweet, or arrogant. The opposite: it's about constantly reviewing your thoughts and others', seeking truth when it's elusive, striving to see reality clearly. It means listening, being aware of and questioning values, and bewaring duplicity, wishful thinking and false perception. We need to keep our minds curious and questing, aware that circumstances change and our understanding develops.

It's also about being real ourselves and not lying to ourselves.

This kind of inner truthfulness is essential for mental health and thus gives well-being a firm foundation. It's useful to do a 'truth review' every now and then, and once you're satisfied that you're doing your best to be true to yourself and others, it gives you a great feeling of oneness with the world as well as personal wholeness.

Deal compassionately with hostility

Living in truth also means that those who like you like the real you and part of your appeal is the honesty, integrity and congruity they subconsciously sense. However it doesn't mean you will get on well with everyone. Yes, you will get on well with those who like and love you and who appreciate and are glad for the person you openly really are and willingly let them know. But there may be some who find your truth troubling because it clashes with their inner dichotomy and in reaction they may turn away from you or even be hostile. That is their story and their journey, not yours. Truth is understanding and compassionate, but it will not turn away from itself or compromise its integrity. Guard it passionately from sabotage and treasure it. Your positive power enables you to do this. It is strong for you, even when you waver. The following exercise is helpful in strengthening and protecting you:

- ✓ Be aware of discord.
- ✓ Ask for help from your subconscious and the greater consciousness.
- ✓ Feel your strength.
- ✓ Breathe deeply.
- ✓ Centre yourself and hold yourself well.
- ✓ Be fair and behave well, with all your integrity.

You are your own consciousness and intelligence. Cling to it determinedly, fiercely, passionately. Your truth is powerful beyond measure – your positivity and the energy that flows from it depends on it. It is the key to your being.

Truth is very, very beautiful. The elixir of freedom of spirit and soul. The essence of life. The essence of you. And the energy of truth is pure and positive.

Know your values and act with integrity

We all have, sometimes without realizing it, a set of values that are important to us. Have you ever thought what yours are? Thinking about it, and clarifying them for yourself is a positive thing to do in itself as it will help you know and understand yourself better. It can also give you valuable insights into those which you might like to prioritize at the moment or develop.

Values are the various positive beliefs you behave by, or try to behave by. Almost any quality that strikes you as a good way to be, which you often incorporate into your personality and life, or aspire to, can be one of your key values. For instance, eagerness, amiability, kindness, love, care, enthusiasm, positivity, serenity, punctuality – but there are so many possibilities and you will know the ones that are yours. Try this exercise:

- ▶ Identify your core beliefs in the best way to live.
- ▶ List them.
- ▶ Then take a look at the whole list and list them again in order of their importance to you at the moment.
- ▶ Consider if you can add to them.
- ▶ Reflect on how good it is to have them as standards in your life.

Many beliefs and life qualities are values we can indeed aspire to – and not just aspire, but wholeheartedly adopt. Optimism, for instance, can be consciously chosen over and above pessimism, and of course this whole book is about the goodness and power of positivity, which again, we can choose and promote, nurture and enjoy to the full so that it becomes a way of life.

Your values, recognized and loved by you, give you a language of behaviour that's easy to follow and live by on a daily basis along with an integrity and wholeness that feels balanced and complete.

Values and integrity, along with the truth they naturally encompass, are an intrinsic part of well-being and a source of both contentment and inspiration. Recognize them, reflect on them often, give thanks for them, look after them and above all, enjoy living by them and up to them. They are gifts given to you and gifts you give to others.

Live ethically and morally

To have an ethos based on integrity and truth and your other positive core values, and live by it intelligently is the basis of wisdom and happiness. 'But being virtuous,' my psychotherapist friend stressed again, 'is not only not easy, it's difficult!'

It's true that behaving well with other individuals, doing the right thing in the wider world too, not causing hurt by your words and actions, and at the same time always being true to yourself and your ethos, can be extremely challenging! It's very easy to give up on it – but please, whenever you are unsure or confused about the right thing to do, keep focused on the reality of the situation and consider different viewpoints on it. That way you will stay positive and find the way through.

Sometimes there is no perfect way that will solve everything and please everyone and then all we can do is our best. Sometimes even our best won't work perfectly or even well. But by doing our best – repeatedly questioning our own motives, morality and integrity using reason, truth and experience so that we are sure it really is our best – we have the confidence of that inner knowledge and honesty that feels so good.

> *The only thing necessary for the triumph of evil is for good men to do nothing.*
>
> Edmund Burke

Morality is active – a living, vibrant thing. Living ethically is never a passive route. Integrity takes commitment and effort. But it buzzes with positivity that gives a steady supply of energy, and when you live ethically and do your best, your own energy flows too, so that it will always be possible and will not even seem hard. It is the right way, the good way and – another blessing – when you make it your way you have a clear conscience and inner peace.

Honour is a wonderful word that's gone somewhat out of fashion now, but the concept still has a special place in our hearts and any civilized, compassionate culture. Behaving honourably, we consider others' well-being and do our best to live alongside them in harmony and mutual respect. Today we are more likely to speak more of having a conscience or scruples, and yes, they are excellent principles too but not exactly the same as honour. Being honourable implies a feel-good sense of being dignified, compassionate and having respect for others and at the same time enjoying and caring for our strong inner sense of right and wrong. There is something about the word and its meaning that when we apply it to ourselves makes us stand up straight, look people in the eye and sense their well-being as well as ours and want to behave well by them at the same time as honouring our own truth. It's inspiring and challenging, and like all things positive, it feels good.

Live humanely

We are fortunate to live in a democracy where every individual is respected and valued and the peace of the country is cherished. Appreciating that, and living following humane principles, we are much blessed. We protest when the system of values most of us live by goes wrong in some way, for instance rebelling against any kind of injustice or unnecessary bureaucracy, and this is very positive, for it helps provide a reality check against corruption and problems. We are currently living in great hope and optimism that the present movement of less fortunate countries towards democracy will continue and that in time life will be fair and good for people of all nations.

Meanwhile we can continue to live positively and lovingly ourselves. What exactly is 'the right way'? It's as helpful to have guidelines for humane living as it is to have your own set of values. You'll find many are the same.

The most quoted tenets of humane living and well-being for all are kindness, mercy, compassion, consideration, tenderness and sympathy for all people and animals. All of these feel great, both in the doing and the receiving, and it's easy to wonder why on earth we don't all live by them, always. But we're human and have a range of negative emotions, traits and weaknesses too which can swing into action in a trice. The trick to remember is to watch out for them and think how to handle them – for sometimes they may actually have a positive and very useful purpose. Anger, for example, can often be a valid, useful indication that something is going wrong and needs constructive attention, but if ignored and allowed to get out of hand it can be dangerously destructive. The humane way is the positive way: to be aware of any emotional negativity that gets in the way of the principles, and think how to deal with it. It's about being aware, taking note, and using reason and thought to figure out the right way we know in our hearts we want to follow. We can also take the energy of anger and use it constructively to strengthen our resolve to behave well towards others. Or perhaps with it we can fire up a new positive plan of action that will in some way make the world a better place.

There are several guides to help us live humanely, well, wisely and kindly. The medical model of ethics is a good starting point:

- ▶ **Remember that everyone is an individual:** This is a lovely way to remember to look for the goodness of others, however obscure. It gives a window to their spirit, and the child they once were. It's also so helpful if ever we find ourselves trying to mould someone else into our way of thinking or being. You're you and they're them. No one else is the same as you, or should be. Just reflecting on this is often all it takes to transmogrify feelings of control or frustration into respect and perhaps acceptance and understanding too. It replaces the negativity of the situation with a welcome feeling of positivity.
- ▶ **Treat everyone humanely and fairly:** When we do this we feel warm and equable. Take ego out of the equation and we naturally do this, so looking beyond yourself and focusing on the other person makes it easy – and a pleasure.
- ▶ **Recognize the right to dignity:** Refusing to take advantage of opportunities to trip someone up or make them look foolish in any way reflects well on you and lets you continue to walk tall yourself, dignified and positive. Everyone's dignity is precious and appreciating and caring for others' as well as our own feels marvellous.
- ▶ **Do no harm:** Tall order this in our complex, delicate, threatened world. Tall order in relationships too. But we're all becoming more and more aware of the need to cherish our loved ones, value others too and protect and nurture as best we can our beautiful world. Thinking positively gives us hope, optimism and also resolve and strength to do right by others, the world and ourselves. To think is the first step: positivity starts with a thought – so think it! With a positive attitude we can change ourselves for the better and make a practical, real positive difference to the world around us and beyond too.

- **Be truthful and honest:** This is vital for everything. I can't stress it enough. We've talked a lot about it already and all the major philosophers have it at the centre of their beliefs too. Live it, think it, sleep it. Feel the positivity and joy.
- **Treat people and other living creatures as you would like to be treated – with respect, love and honesty:** It sounds so obvious, but we need, over and over, to remember to do this – the barometer of your life will be set fair when you do and others will follow your lead.
- **Look out for bad behaviour (your own and others') and be forgiving:** However positively and well we live, we'll still have negative elements and so will others, so we need to be awake to negativity and protect ourselves from it. Positivity is a strong shield which as it protects us also enables us to be fair and forgiving and to look for ways to help ourselves and others behave better. It has huge energy for good.
- **Rejoice in your sense of joy and wonder:** We are so amazingly fortunate to live in this complex, extraordinary world. With the curiosity of a child, practise encouraging and being aware of the awe you feel when you notice something beautiful or fascinating – it puts petty grumbles into perspective and helps us survive the sorrows and traumas of life too. Besides, just in itself it feels so great to stand in awe and wonder! Practise being joyful as often as possible too – it's very much an emotion which, if it's not already a frequent part of your life, you can introduce, and the more you feel it and relish it to the full, the more often it will come to you. This intense feeling of happiness that sweeps over you is healing and energizing and spreads happiness to everyone around you because it's so delightfully infectious. It's great when it's spontaneous, but just as joyful when you encourage it into being; music and dancing, for instance, are a great combination to help you feel the zing of joy running through mind, soul and body, and laughter – especially shared laughter – is an elixir of joy too. Joy and wonder are great gifts – let's give thanks and welcome them heartily.
- **Keep learning:** My dad, a brilliant teacher whose young pupils adored him, used to say: 'Learn at least one new thing a day.' I try to do that still and it's really helpful in recognizing things you've learned that, unnoticed or appreciated, might all too easily be forgotten. Paying attention to anything you've learned – and there

always is something – keeps you interested and interesting. It also reminds us, each day, not just to notice new things we come across, but to actively make and take opportunities to learn. It's such a fabulously complicated, fascinating world, why wouldn't we want to learn more and more and more!

▶ **Respect others' right to have their own opinions:** When you think a lot and form opinions, resist the temptation to insist you are right and anyone who thinks differently must therefore be wrong. Remember that opinions and circumstances can change, and be aware too of the possibility that your thinking may be flawed in any case. So it makes sense and is positive to keep questioning and reviewing your thoughts, opinions and beliefs and to respect others' ideas and of course their right to them.

▶ **Talk through problems:** In any situation, at home, at work and in the world at large, conflicts are best settled by talking, negotiating and compromising. Looking at the situation from everyone's point of view is hugely helpful in clarifying perspectives and also seeing more possibilities for solutions. Remember that concord is never impossible, however diverse the needs of the different parties, and where there is possibility, there is a way to find it. Enjoy the challenge of the search for resolution and harmony and soothe feelings along the way with compassion, understanding and, as ever, respect. It always surprises me how the atmosphere changes from hostility to a willingness to work together to find good ways forward when we remember these values and champion each other's dignity and honour.

▶ **Work together for all people, all other creatures and our world:** We have the intelligence and the means to feed everyone and ensure they have good living conditions, to protect our fellow creatures and to limit the damage we do to the environment and instead care for it zealously and lovingly. If we each do our part as best we can, together we will influence others and the goodwill will promote well-being and accord right around the globe. It's do-able, it's exciting and you and all of us can play our part.

▶ **Recognize and guard against prejudice and discrimination:** Prejudice and the urge to discriminate against certain kinds or groups of people are born of fear – usually fear that they are threatening us in some way and might hurt us, or fear that they are better in some way or have more than we do. All such fear needs to be faced and considered rationally, intelligently and humanely. It can be a great help, when we fear any clan or culture, to remember that each person is a real person, an individual with good and bad points, and probably has friends and family who love them. Prejudice creates hostility, animosity, even rage. It is horribly negative and unconstructive and usually, in some way, actively damaging. It spreads like a rampant virus and can, as history teaches and the present continues to show, be lethal and devastating. Positivity fights for individual respect and dignity, and when we remember this and join the campaign for tolerance, we have inner peace as well as working towards peace and harmony with others.

▶ **Take responsibility for your actions:** Whatever your past, you are free to enjoy life and live well in accordance with your values. You are totally responsible for the way you are from today onwards. Isn't that an inspiring thought? When we blame others and past experiences, it doesn't help the present at all. Certainly, it helps us nurture our well-being and happiness if we recognize how we've arrived where we are now and, with the help of counselling perhaps, let go of bad memories and move on. You have the personal power and integrity to live well and the ability to enjoy life to the full. Take responsibility for your well-being and your autonomy, be glad for it, and feel your positivity as it surges through you.

Whatever our beliefs and whether or not we have a religious faith, the Golden Rule 'Treat others as you would like to be treated' encompasses and is a useful reminder of all the above. If you think about it, it's pure wisdom, isn't it? Try saying it out aloud to yourself and feel all the goodness and love of it.

Live courageously

The minute you remember to think positively you begin to manifest and radiate courage. You perhaps know the feeling when you suddenly get anxious? Often it happens when you wake up during the night or early in the morning. Even the most happy-go-lucky people experience it sometimes; new worries pop up unheralded and old ones get worse, and fear grips. But the extraordinary thing is that the instant you pause to think, and consciously look at them in a positive light, they fall back into perspective. It may be that there's nothing to worry about at all, or, if there is something to cause concern, you see how to deal with it constructively, getting appropriate help if necessary. Instead of having your consciousness taken hostage by fear, your courage is there for you, strong and supportive, along with a full complement of common sense to back it up and give it practicality.

Whether or not we can find immediate solutions to any difficulties and problems that need addressing, we can always summon reserves of strength to see us through. For some people the positive way is to look at the possibilities for how things could pan out, including the very worst scenario, so that they can start forming contingency plans. Others prefer to think positively only about the present and know that they will face the future as it happens and deal with whatever circumstances they find themselves in then. Whatever your preferred approach, awareness of your positive power to cope and survive is there for you, a source of support and strength.

Friends are wonderful at providing a listening ear and empathy, and perhaps some practical advice or help too. Cherish them even when you're feeling at your lowest. They can 'hold' your blues for you for some precious minutes to give you a respite, and if their company helps you raise a smile or laughter that's even better.

Symbolism can help your courage manifest itself too. I remember riding a young ex-racehorse a few years back, rescued because of her wildness. For the first time in my life, I'd lost my nerve on horseback, and the anxiety she was picking up on was making her crazier than ever. As she danced and spooked along a country lane with me aboard feeling increasingly precarious, I was so frightened that I nearly lost it completely. Suddenly I pictured Joan of Arc. Pretending to be her, I loosened the reins and held them in my left hand. I held my right arm straight up in the air as though holding a standard and flag and imagined myself to be full of courage and determination. The mare instantly settled down, walked beautifully and gave me no further cause for worry. A few hundred yards further up the lane, a car was waiting in the middle of the road. The driver looked quizzically at me: 'Why did you tell me to stop?' he asked. He'd taken my arm and aura of purpose to be a command with which he'd naturally complied! If Joan of Arc could have seen the effect her courage had on me, a highly-strung thoroughbred horse and a car driver so many centuries after her life, I'm sure she'd have been delighted! The realization of how the change in my attitude had both positively affected me and the horse inspired me to rethink my relationship with the horse and do some retraining. Soon that wonderful creature and I had complete confidence in each other and for the rest of her life we were great friends.

Now think who inspires *you* with their courage:

- ✓ Picture them in a situation where their bravery is shining through.
- ✓ Sense that you have their courage.
- ✓ Emulate their body language.
- ✓ Imagine you have an aura of confidence.
- ✓ Know that you have the ability and strength to get through.
- ✓ Store this scene and feeling in your memory and use it whenever you need a big injection of courage.
- ✓ Explore avenues to increase your confidence in practical ways to complement your positive attitude.

Live in grace and peace

Life! However much we want to live positively and be good-tempered, enjoy life and be loving to everyone, I bet not even the most saintly person on earth achieves this state all the time! We're always being tested, walking new paths with more conundrums and obstacles for us, coming up against people who seem determined to thwart our best intentions.

But the more positive our attitude generally, the better we weather the storms and negotiate the hurdles and troughs, all the time on an emotional learning curve. And the consequent deepening of character and ever-growing maturity combines with the positivity and enables stretches of sheer happiness and occasional wild peaks of joy and ecstasy. And all the time we're becoming more and more aware of and in touch with the essential joy of life and the sacred sense.

And through the roller-coaster of life, we're growing like plants towards the light of grace and peace, soaking it in and knowing that, like food for the soul, it's life-giving and loving, pure and good.

We're learning as we go, and developing in mind, body and soul, and yes, it's sometimes difficult and life is often problematic one way or another, but goodness it's wonderful and how much more readily we recognize and feel this when we live positively.

Grace is another word we don't use much today but I think it has a special place because it speaks of enlightenment and spiritual contentment. The ideas of both grace and enlightenment tend to be co-opted by various religions that make out that we can only hope to achieve them after decades of prescribed spiritual practice. It's much like the claim that only when we've been meditating for years in a certain way can we do it 'properly'. Here is a wonderful positive revelation: it's perfectly possible to meditate deeply and be fulfilled even as a beginner. And again grace – including enlightenment and spiritual contentment – is a way of being we can experience at any time of our lives.

It's all about the ability to nurture peace deep inside ourselves and radiating all around us, and to be spiritually aware and full of love – really living in the light of love. The reason it's usually assumed or suggested that it takes years of practice is because few feel full of grace until they are much older. But the reason for that is that in our working years, perhaps bringing up a family too and maybe looking after older relatives, we seem so busy and stressed there isn't much time to be spiritually aware and in touch with our inner selves.

In reality there is always time. There is always opportunity. For inner and spiritual awareness and connection constitute a state of being that exists perfectly happily and harmoniously with day-to-day life and complement it well.

You may have tried the exercises throughout this book where you pause to register your being and the positivity and love you feel all around and through you. Let's do it now – and feel the wonder and calm of grace:

- ✓ Pause for a few minutes – or even just moments.
- ✓ Be aware of your whole body.
- ✓ Feel the energy flowing through you.
- ✓ Breathe deeply and sigh.
- ✓ Feel the energy of love, loving you, holding you safe.
- ✓ Register the calm of positivity washing away any stress.

- ✓ Actually or in your mind smile at the greater consciousness.
- ✓ Reach out with your love.
- ✓ Feel the peace within you.

Certainly, the more often we pause and are aware, in a sense tuning in to the other dimensions of love, positivity and peace, the more we'll have the blissful sense of enlightenment. But it's possible any time – a matter of turning towards the light, connecting and being one with love.

Turning towards – that says it all. Just as we turn appreciatively towards our loved ones to look at them, speak with them, and enjoy their company, glad for their presence in our lives, so we can turn towards life and the love and light of our wonderful world.

Live in the light of positivity and bask in goodness, peace and joy.

Light up your life and shine!

Index